# ACROSS THE CURRICULUM

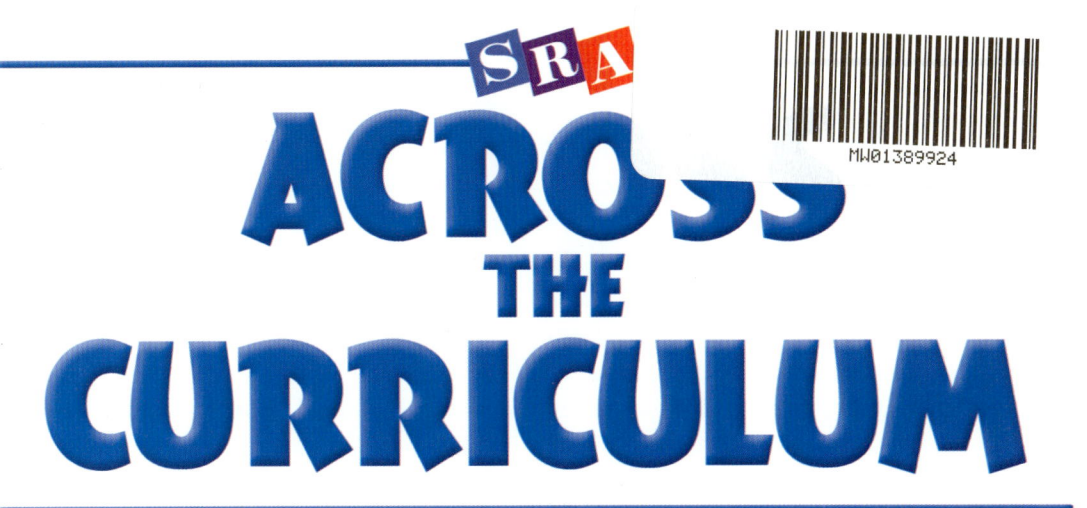

## Math Connections

Grade 3

SRA
Columbus, OH

The McGraw-Hill Companies

# Acknowledgments

*Cover* (c) © Smithsonian American Art Museum/Washington, DC/Art Resource, NY, (tl) © Peter Weber/Getty Images, Inc., (cl) © Gavin Hellier/Getty Images, Inc., (bl) © BrandX Pictures/PictureArts Corporation; *12* © Bernard Photo Productions/Animals Animals - Earth Scenes; *18* © Angelo Cavalli/Getty Images, Inc.; *22* © Bettmann/Corbis; *26* © Image Source/Getty Images, Inc.; *32* © Tony Roberts/Corbis; *38* © Melanie Acevedo/Getty Images, Inc.; *42* © Royalty-Free/Corbis; *46* © Tom Nebbia/Corbis; *52* © Timothy Fadek/Corbis; *56* © Manu Sassoonian/Art Resource, NY; *62* © Photo Alto/Getty Images, Inc.; *68* © Yann Layma/Getty Images, Inc.; *72* © Richard T. Nowitz/Corbis; *78* © Araldo de Luca/Corbis; *82* © PhotoDisc/Getty Images, Inc.; *86* © Digital Vision/Getty Images, Inc.; *92* © PhotoDisc/Getty Images, Inc.; *98* © Alan Majchrowicz/Getty Images, Inc.; *102* © Robert Harding/Getty Images, Inc.; *106* © Kevin Miller/Getty Images, Inc.; *112* © Gary Gay/Getty Images, Inc.; *116* © Richard A. Cooke/Corbis; *122* © Cosmo Condina/Getty Images, Inc.; *128* © W. Cody/Corbis.

The Internet sites referenced here are not under the control of SRA/McGraw-Hill; therefore, SRA makes no representation concerning the content of these sites, their ongoing availability, or links their hosts and/or sponsors may choose to add or delete. We encourage teachers to preview the sites before students access them.

**SRAonline.com**

Copyright © 2007 by SRA/McGraw-Hill.

All rights reserved. Except as permitted under the United States Copyright Act, no part of this publication may be reproduced or distributed in any form or by any means, or stored in a database or retrieval system, without the prior written permission of the publisher, unless otherwise indicated.

Send all inquiries to:
SRA/McGraw-Hill
8787 Orion Place
Columbus, OH 43240-4027

Printed in the United States of America.

ISBN 0-07-603729-0

1 2 3 4 5 6 7 8 9 PHX 10 09 08 07 06

# Table of Contents

**Getting Started** .................................................. 6

| Chapter | Activity | Cross-Curricular Area | Page |
|---|---|---|---|
| 1 **Numbers Concepts**<br>**Math:** Counting and Estimating | 1 **Surface Tension:** Estimate and Compare Amounts<br>**Technology:** Electronic Reference | Science WebQuest | 12 |
| 1 **Number Concepts**<br>**Math:** Numbers to 10,000 | 2 **Poetry:** Write a Poem Using Large Numbers<br>**Technology:** Word Processing | Language Arts | 18 |
| 2 **Multidigit Addition and Subtraction**<br>**Math:** Adding and Subtracting Large Numbers | 1 **Dwellings:** Compare the Cost of Tree Houses<br>**Technology:** Database | Social Studies | 22 |
| 2 **Multidigit Addition and Subtraction**<br>**Math:** Applications of Addition | 2 **Form:** Design a Tree House<br>**Technology:** Spreadsheet | Art WebQuest | 26 |
| 3 **Measuring and Graphing**<br>**Math:** Perimeter and Area | 1 **Cities:** Plan a Garden for an Inner-City Lot<br>**Technology:** Internet | Social Studies WebQuest | 32 |
| 3 **Measuring and Graphing**<br>**Math:** Measuring and Graphing | 2 **Plants:** Research Natural Pest Control<br>**Technology:** Word Processing | Science | 38 |
| 4 **Multiplication Concepts**<br>**Math:** Multiplication and Approximate Measure | 1 **Space:** Design a Dog Park<br>**Technology:** Drawing and Graphics | Art | 42 |
| 4 **Multiplication Concepts**<br>**Math:** Skip Counting | 2 **Informational Text:** Compare Types of Assistance Dogs<br>**Technology:** Presentation | Language Arts WebQuest | 46 |
| 5 **Multiplication and Division Facts**<br>**Math:** Multiplying by 5 and 10 | 1 **Goods:** Edit Images of Appalachian Arts and Crafts<br>**Technology:** Gadgets | Social Studies | 52 |
| 5 **Multiplication and Division Facts**<br>**Math:** Multiplying by 0, 1, and 2 | 2 **Shape and Form:** Create a Presentation about African Art<br>**Technology:** Presentation | Art WebQuest | 56 |
| 6 **Functions**<br>**Math:** Simple Functions | 1 **Simple Machines:** Design Playground Equipment<br>**Technology:** Drawing and Graphics | Science WebQuest | 62 |
| 6 **Functions**<br>**Math:** Applications with Functions | 2 **Fantasy:** Write about a Fantasy Playground<br>**Technology:** Keyboarding | Language Arts | 68 |

ACROSS THE CURRICULUM Math Connections • Table of Contents

| Chapter | Activity | Cross-Curricular Area | Page |
|---|---|---|---|
| **7 Multidigit Multiplication and Division** <br> **Math:** Multiplying by 10, 100, and 1,000 | **1 Economics:** Create a Monetary System <br> **Technology:** Spreadsheet | Social Studies WebQuest | 72 |
| **7 Multidigit Multiplication and Division** <br> **Math:** Applications of Multiplication | **2 Physical Change:** Research Coin Minting <br> **Technology:** Internet | Science | 78 |
| **8 Fractions** <br> **Math:** Fractions of Sets and Numbers | **1 Emphasis:** Create an Advertisement <br> **Technology:** Gadgets | Art | 82 |
| **8 Fractions** <br> **Math:** Halves, Fourths, and Eighths | **2 Examples:** Categorize Toy Advertisements <br> **Technology:** Database | Language Arts WebQuest | 86 |
| **9 Measurement** <br> **Math:** Measuring Elapsed Time | **1 Music:** Evaluate Campfire Songs <br> **Technology:** Computer Basics | Art WebQuest | 92 |
| **9 Measurement** <br> **Math:** Choosing the Correct Unit | **2 Environment:** Plan a Family Camping Trip <br> **Technology:** Word Processing | Science | 98 |
| **10 Decimals** <br> **Math:** Meters and Centimeters | **1 Note Taking:** Research Monuments around the World <br> **Technology:** Electronic Reference | Language Arts | 102 |
| **10 Decimals** <br> **Math:** Scale Drawing with Tenths | **2 Native Americans:** Write about Totem Poles <br> **Technology:** Keyboarding | Social Studies WebQuest | 106 |
| **11 Geometry** <br> **Math:** Polygons | **1 Balance:** Create a Map of Your Neighborhood <br> **Technology:** Drawing and Graphics | Art | 112 |
| **11 Geometry** <br> **Math:** Slides, Flips, and Turns | **2 Descriptive Writing:** Create a Presentation about Houses <br> **Technology:** Presentation | Language Arts WebQuest | 116 |
| **12 Data Analysis and Probability** <br> **Math:** Tally Marks | **1 Animals:** Categorize Sheep Facts <br> **Technology:** Internet | Science WebQuest | 122 |
| **12 Data Analysis and Probability** <br> **Math:** Collecting Data | **2 Careers:** Research Horse Farming <br> **Technology:** Spreadsheet | Social Studies | 128 |

# Teacher Resources

**Mathematic Research Overview** .................................................. 132
    Content Strands of Mathematics ........................................ 132

**Integrating Math with Other Curriculum** ................................ 134
    Integrating Math with Fine Arts ........................................... 134
    Integrating Math with Language Arts ................................. 135
    Integrating Math with Science ............................................ 136
    Integrating Math with Social Studies .................................. 137
    Integrating Math with Technology ...................................... 138

**Technology in the Math Classroom** .......................................... 139

**Technology Guide** ......................................................................... 140
    Computer Basics ................................................................... 140
    Keyboarding .......................................................................... 140
    Word Processing ................................................................... 141
    Drawing and Graphics .......................................................... 141
    Gadgets ................................................................................... 142
    Presentation .......................................................................... 142
    Spreadsheet .......................................................................... 143
    Database ................................................................................ 143
    Electronic Reference ............................................................. 144
    Internet ................................................................................... 144

**Educational Research for Technology** ...................................... 145

**WebQuests** ...................................................................................... 146
    WebQuest History ................................................................ 146
    WebQuest Development ..................................................... 147
    Write Your Own WebQuest ................................................ 148

**eMathTools** ..................................................................................... 150

**Project-Based Learning** ............................................................... 151

**Assessment** ..................................................................................... 152
    How to Evaluate Math .......................................................... 152
    Assessment Samples ............................................................ 153

**Answer Key** ..................................................................................... 158

# Getting Started

## About *Real Math*

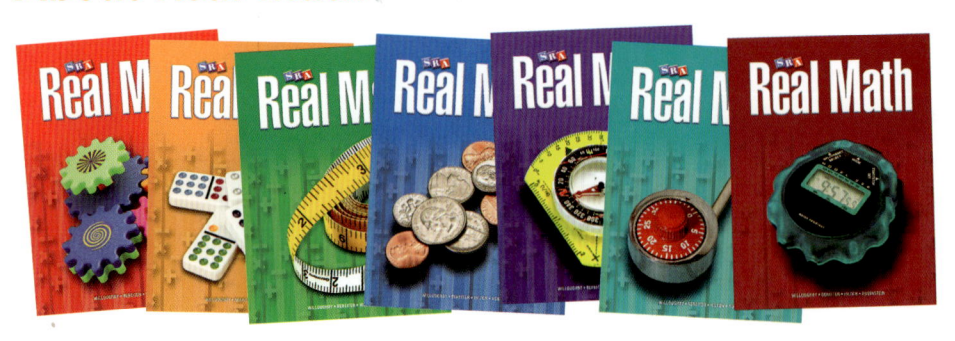

*Real Math* is a comprehensive, elementary-grade, mathematics program designed to

- build mathematical thinking to **reason** about, understand, and **apply** mathematics while identifying, solving, and communicating about real problems.
- teach **basic skills** with **understanding** so they can be used with fluency to solve real problems.
- **engage** students in mathematics so they enjoy math and see it as understandable and useful.

## About *Across the Curriculum Math Connections*

This series of elementary-mathematics applications books provides real-world, true-to-life projects and activities designed to show how mathematics applies to all subject areas.

**Every book includes**
- Language Arts and Reading.
- Science.
- Social Studies.
- Fine Arts.
- Technology.

**Activities are designed to**
- meet grade-level standards in mathematics.
- address grade-level, subject-area standards and guidelines.
- integrate and apply technology.
- build connections, understanding, and critical-thinking skills.

**Each activity includes**
- complete teacher directions, including materials needed and Web resources.
- **Warm-Up** or **Introduction** activities to introduce students to the math and subject-area concepts.
- complete directions for students.
- scoring rubrics for self-assessment and formal assessment.

For more information about *Real Math,* visit the *Real Math* page at *SRAonline.com*.

# How to Use *Across the Curriculum Math Connections*

1. **Choose an activity for students to work on.**
- **Math skills** are aligned with the chapters in the *Real Math* program. Select an activity that supports the skills being taught in math class.
- **Subject-area topics** support units taught in language arts, science, social studies, fine arts, and technology. Select an activity that supports a topic being taught in a main subject area. For a breakdown of the main divisions of subject areas, please refer to pages 8 and 9.
- **Technology** can be used in all the activities, but is required in **WebQuest** activities. Standard activities can be completed without the use of technology. Refer to the Technology Guide on pages 140–144 for more information on how technology is used in *Across the Curriculum Math Connections.*

2. **Choose a grouping for how you want students to work.**
- **Independent Study**   Many standard lessons are designed to be completed by students working independently. The **Warm-Up** blackline master can usually be completed as independent seatwork.
- **Small Group**   The **WebQuest** lessons and some of the standard lessons are designed to be completed by students working in small groups. Often tasks are divided among the students.
- **Whole Class**   Although the projects are predominantly independent or small-group activities, each activity includes opportunities for whole-class discussion. Teachers with one-computer classrooms may adapt the activities to whole-class activities.

3. **Choose a location to determine where students will complete the activity.**
- Math Classroom
- Subject-Area Classroom
- Computer Lab
- Media Center

4. **Choose a time when students will complete the activity.**
- **During Class**   It can be effective to block schedule math, technology, and subject-area classes so that students have extended periods to work on their activities and teachers can team teach.
- **Free or Assigned Center Activity**   Center time is a good way to allow students to complete activities in a one-computer classroom.
- **Before- or After-School Enrichment**   Enrichment or extended-day teachers can support classroom learning by assigning activities.
- **After School**   Families can complete activities together at home, or students can explore activities independently at home.

# Curricular Areas

*Across the Curriculum Math Connections* includes projects and activities from a variety of subject areas.

## Language Arts
The goal of *Across the Curriculum Math Connections* is to connect math to other subjects and to daily life. Students use basic skills fluently to apply mathematics meaningfully to language-arts activities so they can identify, solve, and communicate about real problems. All activities in this book are grounded in the main content strands of mathematics. The language arts activities in this book address a variety of topics in four main subject areas.

- **Personal Writing and Poetry** includes poems, journals, and lists that tell the student's personal story.
- **Narrative Writing** includes sentences, stories, and novels with the components of characters, setting, and plot.
- **Expository Writing** includes definitions, essays, newspapers, and reports that explain, inform, or describe a process.
- **Persuasive Writing** includes reports, letters, and flyers that express an opinion and persuade others to agree with that opinion using facts, statistics, and examples.

## Science
Standards within science and math complement each other. The student can apply mathematical thinking to solve problems within science. The science activities within this book provide students with opportunities for nonstandard mathematical communication in the form of experiments, diagrams, and charts. Purposeful discussion of the projects can lead to mathematical learning. The science activities in this book address a variety of topics in four main subject areas.

- **Life Science** includes the study of living things, life cycles, habitats, and patterns within systems that students can understand through direct observation and quantitative investigation.
- **Earth Science** includes the study of the Earth system and its changes, such as weather, landforms, water forms, and objects in the solar system.
- **Physical Science** includes the study of motion, physical changes in and properties of objects, heat, and light.
- **Health Science** includes the study of the parts of the body and care for the body, such as first aid, nutrition, and disease prevention.

## Social Studies
Social studies activities have natural connections to math. Study of statistical data, maps, and economic systems all meet standards in math and in social studies. The social studies activities in this book address a variety of topics in four main subject areas.

- **Geography** includes the study of characteristics of and the spatial relationships among regions on Earth's surface, as well as human influences on those changes.
- **Civics and Government** includes an understanding of the purpose of rules in the home, school, and community, as well as the roles, rights, and responsibilities of citizens on the local, state, and national levels.
- **Economics** includes an understanding of humans' basic needs and the ways humans meet them as well as an understanding of goods, services, and careers.
- **History and Culture** includes the study of people and their ways of life, both past and present.

**Fine Arts** Fine arts are those arts which result in the creation of aesthetic objects, such as paintings, music, and theatrical performances. Through the integration of math and fine arts, students can understand that the arts and sciences are not separate entities. The fine arts provide an opportunity for students to explore math in nontraditional ways. The fine arts activities in this book address a variety of topics in four main subject areas.

- **Theatre** includes an understanding of plot, character, sound and voice, visual elements, movement, subject, mood, and theme.
- **Music** includes an understanding of musical sound and creative expression, achieved through the use of voice, instruments, musical notation, and appropriate audience behavior.
- **Dance** includes an understanding of movement as a means of creating and communicating meaning.
- **Visual Arts** includes the use of visual structures and functions to express ideas through the use of a variety of materials and processes.

**Technology** Technology is one of the six general principles of mathematics and is essential to teaching and learning mathematics. Technology is used in this book to enhance mathematical thinking, not to replace basic understanding. The technology activities in this book address a variety of topics in ten main subject areas.

- **Computer Basics** includes basic computer operation skills along with computer manners, safety, and ethics.
- **Keyboarding** includes mastering input of letters, symbols, and numbers.
- **Word Processing** includes keying and formatting text.
- **Drawing and Graphics** includes importing and creating graphics.
- **Gadgets** includes peripherals such as printers, scanners, digital cameras, and handhelds.
- **Presentation** includes fundamentals of multimedia presentation software.
- **Spreadsheet** includes analyzing, organizing, and graphing numerical data.
- **Database** includes compiling and analyzing research data.
- **Electronic Reference** includes using technology tools to develop research skills.
- **Internet** includes conducting effective research.

# How to Use the Activities

Each chapter has two types of activities: a standard activity and a **WebQuest** activity.

## Standard Activities

Standard activities can be adapted so that technology is not required to complete the lesson. Standard activities may be individual or group projects.

**Materials** are listed for the activity, including alternative materials for adaptations and Web resources.

**History of Math**, **Profiles in Math**, or **Careers in Math** provide interesting facts related to the subject area and activity.

**Directions** and illustrations are provided to identify and define the necessary steps of the activity.

**Standards** are clearly stated at the end of each activity.

**Objectives** are stated for math, an additional subject area, technology, and Bloom's competencies.

**Prerequisites** are provided to maximize the connections within the activity.

**Additional Applications** give ideas for topics that the activity could support in other subject areas and provides a means of adapting the activity.

**Focus** questions correspond to the objectives of the activity.

**Plan** sections vary with each activity; encourage students to think critically; and may include a graphic organizer, prompts for writing, or space for sketching.

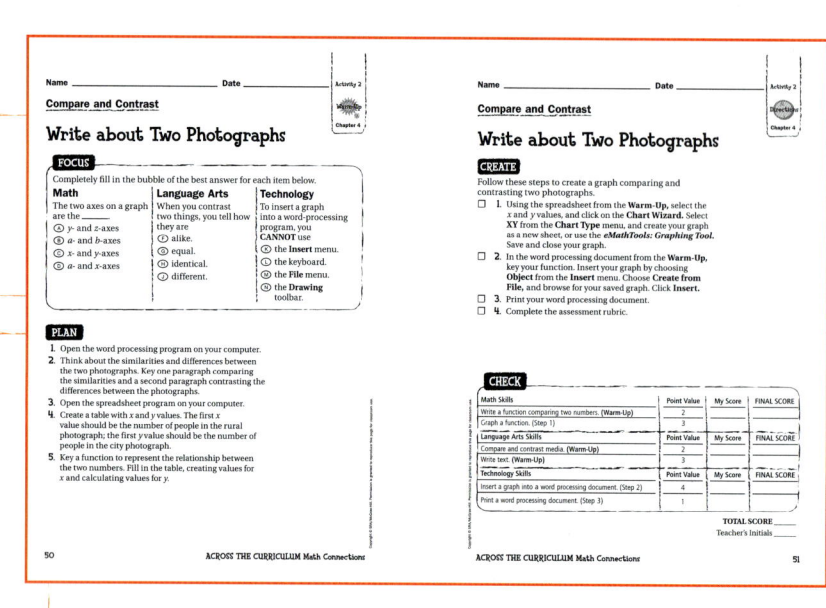

**Create** sections include step-by-step processes for the main activities.

**Check** sections include rubrics that contain math, subject-area, and technology skills for self- and teacher-assessment.

10   Getting Started • ACROSS THE CURRICULUM Math Connections

# WebQuest Activities

**WebQuest** activities require technology and are usually group activities.

**Materials** are listed for the activity, including alternative materials for adaptations and Web resources.

**History of Math, Profiles in Math,** or **Careers in Math** provide interesting facts related to the subject area and activity.

**Objectives** are stated for math, an additional subject area, technology, and Bloom's competencies.

**Prerequisites** are provided to maximize the connections within the activity.

**Additional Applications** give ideas for topics that the activity could support in other subject areas and provides a means of adapting the activity.

**Directions** and illustrations are provided to identify and define the necessary steps of the activity.

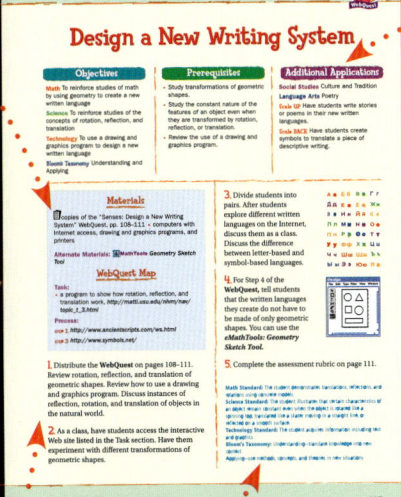

**Standards** are clearly stated at the end of each activity.

**Introduction** pages provide background material to the students and create interest in the activity.

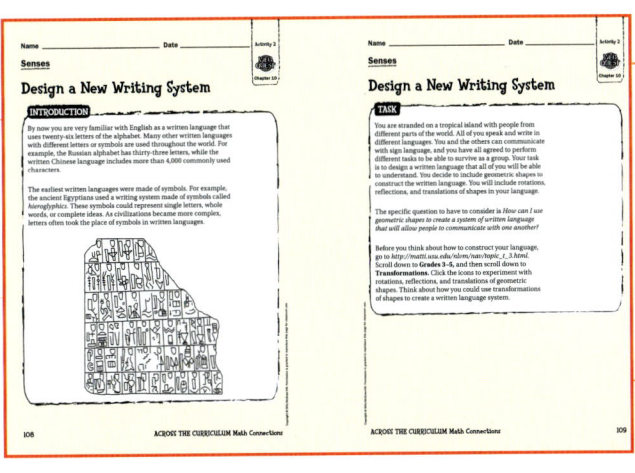

**Task** pages explain what is expected of the students, communicate the central question around which the **WebQuest** is designed, and may outline the role of the student or the scenario of the **WebQuest**.

**Process** pages guide the students through the main activity with step-by-step instructions.

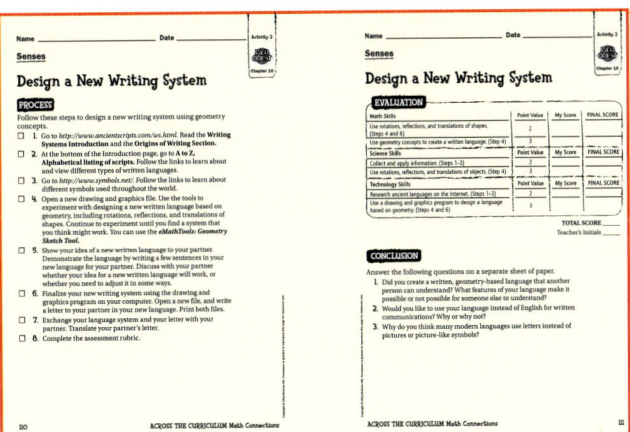

**Evaluation** sections include rubrics that contain math, subject-area, and technology skills for self- and teacher-assessment.

**Conclusion** sections pose questions that enable students to reflect upon the projects and provide input.

ACROSS THE CURRICULUM Math Connections • Getting Started

11

## Activity 1

### Careers in Math

**W**ater tension allows certain insects to skate over the surface of the water. Detergents in many cleaners, however, destroy the bond that creates surface tension. When detergents get in lakes, they break surface tension and disrupt the lives of aquatic insects. Environmental scientists have proved that a very small amount of detergent can cause this disruption. They use science and math to show people how dangerous water pollution can be.

Surface Tension **SCIENCE WebQuest**

# Estimate and Compare Amounts

## Objectives

**Math** To reinforce applications of counting and estimating by performing a science experiment

**Science** To reinforce studies of surface tension by experimenting with drops of water on a penny

**Technology** To use electronic reference resources to research the surface tension of water

**Bloom's Taxonomy** Understanding and Analyzing

## Prerequisites

- Practice counting and estimating numbers of objects.
- Review how surface tension works.
- Review how to search a reference CD-ROM for information.

## Additional Applications

**Fine Arts** Shape
**Social Studies** Environmental Issues
**Scale UP** Have groups repeat the experiment using alcohol and other types of liquid.
**Scale BACK** Have students perform the experiment as a class.

## Materials

copies of the "Surface Tension: Estimate and Compare Amounts" WebQuest, pp. 14–17
• computers with Internet access and CD-ROM drives • science reference CD-ROMs • cups of water • paper clips • paper towels • eye droppers • pennies • paper • pencils

## WebQuest Map

**Task:**
"Sticky Water," an article explaining surface tension in water,
http://www.exploratorium.edu/ronh/bubbles/sticky_water.html

**Process:**

STEP 2 http://www.tangenttoy.com/about.html

STEP 3 http://pbskids.org/zoom/activities/sci/floatingpaperclips.html

STEP 4 http://www.szgdocent.org/resource/ff/f-wtrbg.htm

**1.** Distribute the **WebQuest** on pages 14–17. Review how to estimate and compare amounts in real-life situations. Discuss the concept of surface tension. Review how to search a reference CD-ROM.

**2.** Find the online article "Sticky Water." Read it aloud, and have students discuss examples of surface tension in water and in other liquids.

**3.** Some CD-ROMs require simple installation to run. Complete the installation before class. Reference CD-ROMs offer different types of multimedia features. Preview software before student use so you know the types of available media.

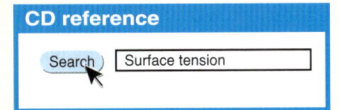

**4.** Divide students into small groups. Distribute the materials.

**5.** Allow students to share their results. Complete the assessment rubric on page 17.

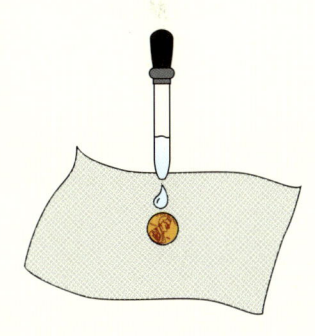

**Math Standard:** The student estimates to determine reasonable results.
**Science Standard:** The student knows that matter has physical properties.
**Technology Standard:** The student applies appropriate electronic search strategies in the acquisition of information including key word search strategies.
**Bloom's Taxonomy:** Understanding—discuss and restate ideas from research
Analyzing—use research and life experience to predict experiment results

**CHAPTER 1 Number Concepts • Surface Tension**

Name _____ Date _____

Activity 1

**Surface Tension**

# Estimate and Compare Amounts

**WEB QUEST**
Chapter 1

## INTRODUCTION

If you have ever seen drops of rain fall on a leaf, you have probably noticed they look like little beads. You may have wondered why water does not simply lie flat. Drops of water form beads because of something called *surface tension*. Surface tension is caused by the action of water molecules. Molecules are the smallest whole part of a substance such as water. The molecules on the surface of water pull each other together to form a stretchy "skin." When there is only a small amount of water, the pull of the molecules is so strong that the water is pulled into a ball. You will research to find out more about surface tension and perform an experiment in which you will estimate and compare amounts.

ACROSS THE CURRICULUM Math Connections

Name _____ Date _____

**Activity 1**
**WEB QUEST**
**Chapter 1**

**Surface Tension**

# Estimate and Compare Amounts

> **TASK**
>
> You are part of a group of scientists who work for a children's science center. You have been assigned the job of creating an interactive exhibit about surface tension. Children will be able to drop water onto pennies to test how many drops it takes to break the surface tension. You will first research and explore surface tension and its use in toy design and in nature. You will then estimate how many water drops can be put on a penny and test your hypothesis.
>
> The specific question you have to consider is *How many drops of water can be put on a penny before the surface tension breaks?*
>
> Before you begin your research, listen as your teacher reads the article "Sticky Water." Discuss examples of surface tension that you have seen.

ACROSS THE CURRICULUM Math Connections

Name _____ Date _____

Activity 1
WEB QUEST
Chapter 1

**Surface Tension**

# Estimate and Compare Amounts

**PROCESS**

Follow these steps to estimate and compare amounts.

☐ 1. Use at least two electronic reference sources, such as encyclopedia CD-ROMs, to research surface tension.

☐ 2. Go to *http://www.tangenttoy.com/about.html,* and listen as your teacher reads it aloud. Write down how this inventor uses science to make toys.

☐ 3. Go to *http://pbskids.org/zoom/activities/sci/floatingpaperclips.html.* Using the materials your teacher provides, perform this simple experiment. See if you can get the paper clip to float without using the paper towel.

☐ 4. Go to *http://www.szgdocent.org/resource/ff/f-wtrbg.htm,* and read about the different aquatic insects. Write down how the water's surface tension affects them.

☐ 5. Take an eye dropper, and put it into a cup of water. Squeeze the bulb to fill it with water. Set a penny on a paper towel. Hold the dropper about a centimeter above the penny's center, and squeeze it. Record what happens to the water.

☐ 6. As a group, estimate how many drops you think you can put on the penny before the water spills onto the paper towel. Test your estimate. Experiment with dropping water onto the edges instead of the center of the penny. Record what happens.

☐ 7. Write a paragraph comparing your estimate with the actual results. Share it with the class.

☐ 8. Complete the assessment rubric.

ACROSS THE CURRICULUM Math Connections

Name _____ Date _____

Activity 1

**Surface Tension**

WEB QUEST
Chapter 1

# Estimate and Compare Amounts

## EVALUATION

| Math Skills | Point Value | My Score | FINAL SCORE |
|---|---|---|---|
| Estimate the amount of water drops that break surface tension. (Step 6) | 2 | | |
| Measure the actual amount of water drops that break surface tension. (Step 6) | 3 | | |
| **Science Skills** | **Point Value** | **My Score** | **FINAL SCORE** |
| Research scientific information on surface tension. (Steps 1–4) | 2 | | |
| Formulate and test a hypothesis. (Step 6) | 3 | | |
| **Technology Skills** | **Point Value** | **My Score** | **FINAL SCORE** |
| Enter a URL and view a Web page. (Steps 2–4) | 1 | | |
| Search a CD-ROM for information. (Step 1) | 4 | | |

**TOTAL SCORE** _____

Teacher's Initials _____

## CONCLUSION

Answer the following questions on a separate sheet of paper.

1. How many water drops did you estimate that the penny would hold? What was the actual number?

2. What did you learn about surface tension during this **WebQuest**?

ACROSS THE CURRICULUM Math Connections

17

# Activity 2

## History of Math

**A**ncient cultures varied in how they viewed large numbers. The ancient Greek number system went to only 10,000, while the early Roman number system had no symbols or terms for numbers above 100,000. However, India, which had a more advanced number system, had names for each of the powers of 10 up to $10^{12}$, as early as the third century A.D.

# Write a Poem Using Large Numbers

## Objectives

**Math** To reinforce studies of numbers to 10,000 by using large numbers in a poem

**Language Arts** To reinforce studies of poetry by writing a group poem

**Technology** To use a word processing program to key a group poem and change font attributes

**Bloom's Taxonomy** Applying and Creating

## Prerequisites

- Practice solving problems with numbers to 10,000.
- Practice writing various types of poetry, including group poems.
- Review how to use a word processing program.

## Additional Applications

**Social Studies** Distance
**Fine Arts** Unity
**Scale UP** Have students research statistics on a specific topic and write a poem using the statistics.
**Scale BACK** Have students write a poem using numbers to 100.

## Materials

copies of the "Poetry: Write a Poem Using Large Numbers" Warm-Up and Directions, pp. 20 and 21 • computers with word processing programs and printers • paper • pencils

## Web Resources

- http://www.teachingandlearningresources.co.uk/numbers.shtml
- http://cla.univ-fcomte.fr/english/index_s.htm
- http://www.onlinepoetryclassroom.org/index.cfm

1. Complete the **Warm-Up** activity on page 20. Review numbers to 10,000, and discuss things that come in large quantities or that are measured in large numbers. Discuss how poetry may be written in groups. Review how to use a word processing program.

2. Assign students to groups of three or four. Have each group choose one topic about which to write their poem. The topic should be related to numbers to 10,000. Possible topics include distances, amounts of people, and so on.

3. Distribute the **Directions** on page 21. Have students take turns writing lines for their group's poem. Students should decide on a final version of their poem. Remind them to use large numbers in their poem.

4. Have students use a word processing program to key their poem. Demonstrate how to change font attributes, such as style, size, and color, to complement the appearance of their poem. If computer access is not available, have students write the final version on paper.

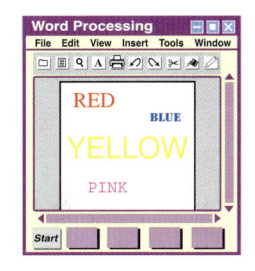

5. Have students print a copy of their poem for each person in the group. Have each group share their poem with the class, with each student reading part of the poem.

6. Complete the assessment rubric on page 21.

**Math Standard:** The student uses place value to read, write (in symbols and words), and describe the value of whole numbers through 999,999.
**Language Arts Standard:** The student writes in different forms for different purposes such as lists to record, letters to invite or thank, and stories or poems to entertain.
**Technology Standard:** The student uses appropriate software to express ideas including the use of word processing.
**Bloom's Taxonomy:** Applying—use numbers to 10,000 in a poem
Creating—produce a group poem

CHAPTER 1 Number Concepts • Poetry

Name _____ Date _____  Activity 2

**Poetry**

Warm-Up
Chapter 1

# Write a Poem Using Large Numbers

**FOCUS**

Completely fill in the bubble of the best answer for each item below.

**Math**
In the number 8,462, _____ is in the thousands place.

Ⓐ 6
Ⓑ 8
Ⓒ 4
Ⓓ 2

**Language Arts**
A group poem is written by

Ⓕ two or more people.
Ⓖ a teacher and a student.
Ⓗ one person.
Ⓙ students only.

**Technology**
To key numbers in a word processing program, you can use

Ⓚ the number keys and the Shift key.
Ⓛ the function keys.
Ⓜ the letter keys and the Control key.
Ⓝ the number keys.

**PLAN**

1. Think of things that come in large quantities or that are measured in large numbers. Record your ideas in the appropriate boxes below.

| 1–99 | 100–999 | 1,000–10,000 |
|---|---|---|
|  |  |  |

2. Choose one of your ideas from the *100–999* or *1,000–10,000* box to write a poem.

3. On a separate piece of paper, use a web to brainstorm ideas for your poem. Think about how you can use large numbers in your poem.

Name _____  Date _____  Activity 2

**Poetry**

Directions

Chapter 1

# Write a Poem Using Large Numbers

**CREATE**

Follow these steps to write a group poem using large numbers.

☐ 1. As a group, talk about the topic you chose for your poem. Write down ideas for your poem.

☐ 2. One person in your group should write the first line of the poem on a piece of paper. Then each person should take turns writing a line of the poem.

☐ 3. Read your finished poem. Make any changes that you want. Decide on a final version of your poem. Give your poem a title.

☐ 4. Open the word processing program on your computer. Take turns keying your poem.

☐ 5. Change font styles, sizes, and colors by selecting parts of your poem and choosing **Options** from the Formatting toolbar.

☐ 6. Print a copy of your poem for each person in your group. Share your poem with the class.

☐ 7. Complete the assessment rubric.

**CHECK**

| Math Skills | Point Value | My Score | FINAL SCORE |
|---|---|---|---|
| Work with numbers to 10,000. (Step 1) | 5 | | |
| **Language Arts Skills** | Point Value | My Score | FINAL SCORE |
| Write a group poem. (Steps 2 and 3) | 5 | | |
| **Technology Skills** | Point Value | My Score | FINAL SCORE |
| Key text and change font attributes in a word processing program. (Steps 4 and 5) | 5 | | |

TOTAL SCORE _____

Teacher's Initials _____

ACROSS THE CURRICULUM Math Connections

### Activity 1

## History of Math

In 1952, RCA developed Bizmac, a computer with an iron-core (or main) memory and a magnetic drum. This computer supported the first database. It could store data about one subject on as many as two hundred magnetic tapes. In the 1960s, IBM began to research the idea of relational databases to automate office functions. Relational databases use relational calculus and algebra to allow users with little technical knowledge to store and retrieve large amounts of information.

**Dwellings** — SOCIAL STUDIES

# Compare the Cost of Tree Houses

## Objectives

**Math** To reinforce studies of addition and subtraction by adding and subtracting prices

**Social Studies** To reinforce studies of dwellings by researching tree houses

**Technology** To use a database program to create a database about tree houses

**Bloom's Taxonomy** Creating and Analyzing

## Prerequisites

- Practice adding and subtracting large numbers.
- Study how dwellings relate to the cultures in which they are found.
- Review how to use a database program.

## Additional Applications

**Language Arts** Informational Text
**Science** Basic Needs
**Scale UP** Have students include prices for all the details of the tree house and include a list of tools needed to build the tree house.
**Scale BACK** Have students work in groups, and give students lists of materials and their prices.

## Materials

copies of the "Dwellings: Compare the Cost of Tree Houses" Warm-Up and Directions, pp. 24 and 25 • computers with Internet access, word processing programs, and database programs • paper • pencils • rulers

**Alternate Materials:** advertisements showing costs for materials • books about tree houses

## Web Resources

- http://pages.areaguides.com/ubuild/TreeHouse.htm
- http://www.thetreehouseguide.com/
- http://www.verifiedsoftware.com/goodturns/woodcosts.htm
- http://familyfun.go.com/decoratingideas/building/feature/famf0602_proj_treehouse/

**1.** Have students complete the **Warm-Up** activity on page 24. Practice adding and subtracting large numbers. Review and discuss various types of dwellings. Review how to use a database program. Have students look at pictures of tree houses on the Internet or in books for ideas.

**2.** Distribute the **Directions** on page 25. For Step 3, have students plan the amount of materials they will need using 12-inch long 2 × 2 pieces of lumber and 2 × 8 pieces of plywood. Have students use Web sites or advertisements to find out costs of materials. Have them round costs to the nearest dollar.

**3.** Students will have trouble calculating the amount of materials needed. Help students break down the tree house by walls, roof, and base. Draw a diagram on the board to help students visualize the different pieces of the tree house.

**4.** For Step 3, have students research various Web sites to get different costs of materials for a comparison of prices.

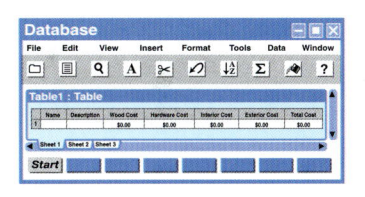

**5.** For Step 7, copy each record to make a class database.

**6.** Complete the assessment rubric on page 25.

**Math Standard:** The student adds and subtracts to solve meaningful problems involving whole numbers.
**Social Studies Standard:** The student uses problem-solving and decision-making skills, working independently and with others, in a variety of settings.
**Technology Standard:** The student uses appropriate software to solve problems including the use of databases.
**Bloom's Taxonomy:** Creating—generate a design for a tree house
Analyzing—determine the materials needed for a tree house

CHAPTER 2 Multidigit Addition and Subtraction • Dwellings

Name _____ Date _____

**Dwellings**

Activity 1
Warm-Up
Chapter 2

# Compare the Cost of Tree Houses

**FOCUS**

Completely fill in the bubble of the best answer for each item below.

**Math**

Which tree house costs the least given the materials provided?

Ⓐ wood: $345; hardware: $20; other: $55

Ⓑ wood: $425; hardware: $10; other: $25

Ⓒ wood: $230; hardware: $40; other: $75

Ⓓ wood: $518; hardware: $15; other: $125

**Social Studies**

Which is **NOT** a kind of dwelling?

Ⓕ apartment
Ⓖ tree house
Ⓗ hut
Ⓙ bed

**Technology**

For which of the following would you **NOT** use a database?

Ⓚ drawing pictures of data
Ⓛ organizing data
Ⓜ storing data
Ⓝ sorting data

**PLAN**

1. Look at the tree house to the right. Think about what materials you would use to build that tree house.

2. Write down the amount of materials you think it would take to build the tree house.

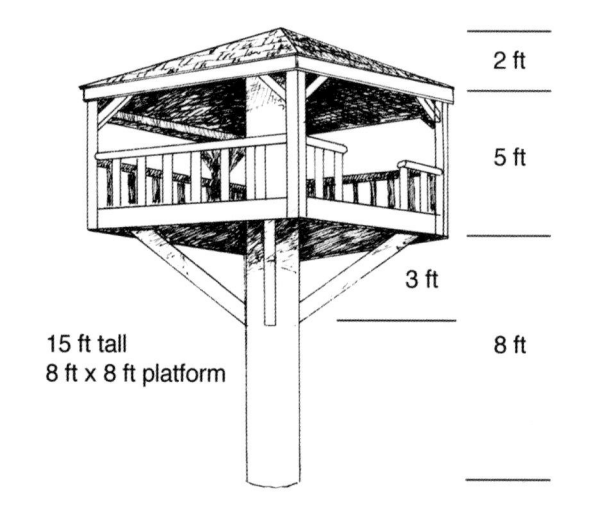

15 ft tall
8 ft x 8 ft platform

2 ft
5 ft
3 ft
8 ft

24

ACROSS THE CURRICULUM Math Connections

Name _____ Date _____

*Activity 1*

**Dwellings**

*Directions*

*Chapter 2*

# Compare the Cost of Tree Houses

**CREATE**

Follow these steps to compare the cost of tree houses.

☐ 1. In a word processing program, list the materials you would need to build a tree house, such as wood, nails, shingles, hinges, and so on. Calculate the amount of materials needed to build the tree house.

☐ 2. Research the costs for the materials. Be sure to estimate the costs for the correct sizes of wood.

☐ 3. Key a description of your tree house in the first field.

☐ 4. List the materials you need in your database by group. For example, *wood* would be one group.

☐ 5. Enter the costs in the database. Add the costs to get a total cost for the tree house materials. Enter the total cost.

☐ 6. Put all data together in a class database. Compare the costs.

☐ 7. Complete the assessment rubric.

**CHECK**

| Math Skills | Point Value | My Score | FINAL SCORE |
|---|---|---|---|
| Find the amount of materials needed and costs. (Steps 1, 2, and 5) | 5 | | |
| **Social Studies Skills** | **Point Value** | **My Score** | **FINAL SCORE** |
| Determine what features are needed for a tree house dwelling. (Step 1) | 5 | | |
| **Technology Skills** | **Point Value** | **My Score** | **FINAL SCORE** |
| Enter information into a database. (Steps 3-5) | 5 | | |

**TOTAL SCORE** _____

Teacher's Initials _____

ACROSS THE CURRICULUM Math Connections

**Activity 2**

## Careers in Math

**A**rchitects design buildings, but they also must figure out what materials will be needed to construct their designs, and they use math to estimate the building costs. They also solve problems. For example, an architect might be asked to design a tree house that can be used by people in wheelchairs. Architects blend together their clients' needs and wants with their own ideas and creativity.

Form

# Design a Tree House

## Objectives

**Math** To reinforce applications of addition by adding lumber prices

**Fine Arts** To reinforce studies of the element of form by constructing a model of a tree house

**Technology** To use a spreadsheet program to calculate lumber prices for a tree house

**Bloom's Taxonomy** Analyzing and Creating

## Prerequisites

- Practice adding and subtracting prices.
- Review the element of form.
- Review how to use the AutoSum feature in a spreadsheet program.

## Additional Applications

**Science** Conservation

**Language Arts** Collaborative Writing

**Scale UP** Have students create scale models of their tree houses.

**Scale BACK** Have students plan tree house designs using only one size of lumber.

## Materials

copies of the "Form: Design a Tree House" WebQuest, pp. 28–31 • computers with Internet access and spreadsheet programs • drawing paper • pencils • rulers • craft sticks • nontoxic glue

## WebQuest Map

**Task:**
"Tree Houses Take a Bough," an article from the Smithsonian Magazine about the growing popularity of tree houses,
**http://www.smithsonianmag.si.edu/smithsonian/issues97/aug97/treehouses.html**

**Process:**

STEP 1 *http://www.danielswoodland.com/ExtremeTreehouses.htm*

STEP 2 *http://www.treehouses.org/*

STEP 3 *http://www.thetreehouseguide.com/building.htm*

STEP 4 *http://www.greenbuilder.com/sourcebook/DimensionalLumber.html*

1. Distribute the **WebQuest** on pages 28–31. Review addition and subtraction. Discuss aspects of the element of form. Demonstrate for students how to enter information in a spreadsheet and how to use the AutoSum feature to add numbers in a column.

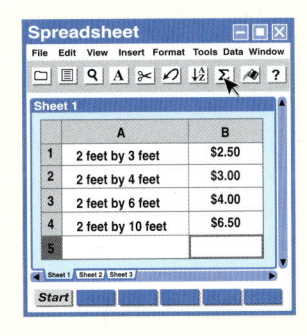

2. Find the article "Tree Houses Take a Bough." Read it aloud, and have students discuss the appeal of tree houses to people of all ages.

3. Divide students into groups. Some of the Web sites contain text that is above level; look over the Web sites ahead of time, and read text aloud when appropriate.

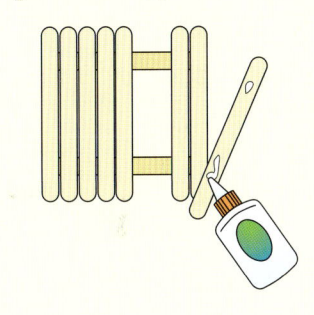

4. Students may need help understanding the different sizes of lumber typically available. Draw diagrams on the board to help students visualize the boards. For Step 6 of the **WebQuest,** you may help students locate prices on the Internet.

5. Have students share their designs with the class.

6. Complete the assessment rubric on page 31.

**Math Standard:** The student models addition and subtraction using pictures, words, and numbers.

**Fine Arts Standard:** The student produces drawings, paintings, prints, constructions, ceramics, and fiber art, using a variety of art materials appropriately.

**Technology Standard:** The student uses appropriate software to solve problems including the use of spreadsheets.

**Bloom's Taxonomy:** Analyzing—determine the amount of lumber needed to construct a tree house
Creating—incorporate ideas from research in a tree house design

**CHAPTER 2 Multidigit Addition and Subtraction • Form** 27

Name _____ Date _____

**Activity 2**

**Form**

# Design a Tree House

> **INTRODUCTION**
>
> In modern America, most tree houses are built as play areas for children, but tree houses have been used as real homes for hundreds of years. In the eighteenth century, the explorer Captain Cook found the people of Tasmania living in tree houses. The Korowai of West Papua live in tree houses that are six to fifty meters off the ground. You will learn about different types of tree houses and design a tree house of your own.

28　　ACROSS THE CURRICULUM Math Connections

Name _____ Date _____

Activity 2

**Form**

# Design a Tree House

> **TASK**
>
> You are working with a group of architects. A family wants you to design a tree house for their children, and they want it to include interesting and fun features. They also want you to figure out how much the lumber will cost. You will first research tree houses and ways of designing a tree house. You will then design a tree house, figure out what lumber is needed, and make a spreadsheet calculating the cost. Finally, you will build a small model of the tree house.
>
> The specific question you have to consider is *How much would it cost to buy wood to build a creative tree house?*
>
> Before you begin your research, listen as your teacher reads the article "Tree Houses Take a Bough." Discuss why different types of people like tree houses.

ACROSS THE CURRICULUM Math Connections

Name _____  Date _____

**Form**

Activity 2

**WEB QUEST**

Chapter 2

# Design a Tree House

**PROCESS**

Follow these steps to design a tree house.

☐ 1. Go to *http://www.danielswoodland.com/ExtremeTreehouses.htm*. Click the images to read more about tree houses. Take notes.

☐ 2. Go to *http://www.treehouses.org/*. Read about Forever Young Treehouses and its mission to build tree houses anyone can use. Click links under *Treehouse Folios* to see examples of tree houses. Discuss how you could make your tree house usable for anyone.

☐ 3. Go to *http://www.thetreehouseguide.com/building.htm*. Listen as your teacher reads aloud. Take detailed notes about building a tree house.

☐ 4. Go to *http://www.greenbuilder.com/sourcebook/DimensionalLumber.html*. Listen as your teacher reads the article "Dimensional Lumber," and take notes.

☐ 5. Use rulers and pencils to create a design for your tree house. Decide how big the tree will be. Use the information about lumber dimensions to plan the house's basic measurements. Figure out how much of each size lumber you will need.

☐ 6. Research the prices for your wood. Choose wood, such as cedar, that will last outside.

☐ 7. Open a new spreadsheet document. Label two columns for *lumber* and *price*. For each piece of lumber you need to buy, key in its size and its price. Use the AutoSum feature to find the total price for lumber. Check the answer.

☐ 8. Use craft sticks to construct a rough model of your tree house.

☐ 9. Share your designs with the class.

☐ 10. Complete the assessment rubric.

Name _____  Date _____

Activity 2

**Form**

Web Quest — Chapter 2

# Design a Tree House

## EVALUATION

| Math Skills | Point Value | My Score | FINAL SCORE |
|---|---|---|---|
| Create a list of lumber prices. (Step 7) | 2 | | |
| Calculate the sum of the prices. (Step 7) | 3 | | |

| Fine Arts Skills | Point Value | My Score | FINAL SCORE |
|---|---|---|---|
| Design a tree house. (Step 5) | 2 | | |
| Build a three-dimensional model of the tree house. (Step 8) | 3 | | |

| Technology Skills | Point Value | My Score | FINAL SCORE |
|---|---|---|---|
| Enter a URL and view a Web page. (Steps 1–4) | 1 | | |
| Create a spreadsheet and use the AutoSum feature. (Step 7) | 4 | | |

**TOTAL SCORE** _____

Teacher's Initials _____

## CONCLUSION

Answer the following questions on a separate sheet of paper.

1. What was the total cost of lumber for your tree house?
2. If you could add one more thing to your tree house, what would it be?
3. What was the most challenging part of this **WebQuest?** Why?

ACROSS THE CURRICULUM Math Connections

**Activity 1**

## Careers in Math

**L**andscape architects design landscapes for residences, offices, parks, playgrounds, and golf courses. Their goal is to make these spaces functional, attractive, and compatible with the natural environment. They plan the location of buildings, roads, and walkways. They analyze the natural elements of the site, such as the climate, soil, slope of the land, drainage, and vegetation. Also they assess the effect of existing buildings, roads, walkways, and utilities on the project.

Cities — SOCIAL STUDIES WebQuest

# Plan a Garden for an Inner-City Lot

## Objectives

**Math** To reinforce studies of perimeter and area by measuring the perimeter and calculating the area of a garden lot

**Social Studies** To reinforce studies of cities in modern society by researching community gardens

**Technology** To use the Internet for research

**Bloom's Taxonomy** Creating and Analyzing

## Prerequisites

- Practice measuring perimeter and calculating area.
- Study the idea of community in an urban culture.
- Review the use of the Internet to find information.

## Additional Applications

**Language Arts** Persuasive Writing

**Science** Soil

**Scale UP** Have students consider more sophisticated aspects of landscape design such as drainage and light sources.

**Scale BACK** Have students create less complex designs with fewer features.

## Materials

copies of the "Cities: Plan a Garden for an Inner-City Lot" WebQuest, pp. 34–37 • computers with Internet access • books of garden plans • graph paper • pencils • rulers • colored pencils

## WebQuest Map

**Task:**
Web site about how to turn a vacant lot into an urban garden,
http://www.greentreks.org/allprograms/roughterrain/urbangardening/howto.asp

**Process:**

STEP 1 http://www.openlands.org/urbangreening.asp?pgid=108

STEP 2 http://celosangeles.ucdavis.edu/garden/articles/startup_guide.html

STEP 3 http://www.usna.usda.gov/Hardzone/

STEP 4 http://www.garden.org/foodguide/browse

**1.** Distribute the **WebQuest** on pages 34–37. Practice measuring perimeter and calculating area. Study the idea of community and community gardens. Review how to enter a URL and view a Web site.

**2.** Discuss as a class some reasons for turning a vacant lot into a community garden.

**3.** For Steps 1 and 2 of the **WebQuest,** have students review the Web site documents as a class. Discuss key aspects of community garden development.

**4.** For Step 7, remind students that they need to think about watering plants, adding walkways, and addressing safety issues.

**5.** For Step 8, help students create a scale. Have students find the perimeter and calculate the area of the various parts of their garden and compare their measurements to real-life spaces.

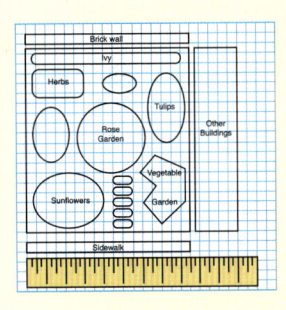

**6.** Complete the assessment rubric on page 37.

**Math Standard:** The student selects and uses appropriate units and procedures to measure length and area.

**Social Studies Standard:** The student describes the effects of physical and human processes in shaping the landscape.

**Technology Standard:** The student uses a variety of strategies to acquire information from electronic resources, with appropriate supervision.

**Bloom's Taxonomy:** Creating—plan a garden design
Analyzing—determine what elements are needed in a design

CHAPTER 3 Measuring and Graphing • Cities

Name _____ Date _____

**Activity 1**

**Cities**

# Plan a Garden for an Inner-City Lot

## INTRODUCTION

People create community gardens by transforming land into community green spaces. These spaces have plants, vegetables, flowers, sitting areas, and playgrounds. They can be created on vacant lots or the grounds of apartment buildings, community centers, or other buildings where people share land and other resources. Urban community gardening is growing in the United States. There are more than 15,000 organized community gardens. The gardens often are created when local residents grow tired of vacant land, trash, and crime in their communities. The residents take control of the land and design and maintain the garden. The gardens are places for neighbors to meet and relax in their community. The gardens also provide green spaces in densely populated urban neighborhoods.

For this activity, you are going to research community gardens. You will use the Internet to research what is needed to create a community garden. You will then design your own community garden.

Name _____ Date _____

**Activity 1**

**Cities**

# Plan a Garden for an Inner-City Lot

**WEB QUEST**
**Chapter 3**

> **TASK**
>
> You live in a big city. You have just overheard that there is a vacant lot close to where you live. You have an idea to convert the vacant lot into a community garden. Your task is to research community gardens. You will learn about some ideas for how to create gardens. Then you will develop a design for your own garden. You will use real measurements and design elements.
>
> The specific question you have to consider is *What will my community garden include?*
>
> Before you begin your individual research, go to *http://www.greentreks.org/allprograms/roughterrain/urbangardening/howto.asp,* and read some basic ideas about how you can turn a vacant lot into a community garden.

ACROSS THE CURRICULUM Math Connections    35

Name _____  Date _____

**Activity 1**

**WEB QUEST**

**Chapter 3**

## Cities

# Plan a Garden for an Inner-City Lot

### PROCESS

Follow these steps to research and design a garden on a vacant lot.

☐ 1. Go to *http://www.openlands.org/urbangreening.asp?pgid=108*. Read about how to start a community garden. Write down the steps. Write down any notes to help you plan the garden design.

☐ 2. Go to *http://celosangeles.ucdavis.edu/garden/articles/startup_guide.html*. Read more about how to start a community garden. Add to your list anything else that you need to think about for a garden design.

☐ 3. Search the Internet for a plan of a community garden. Look in books to find other community garden plans.

☐ 4. Go to *http://www.usna.usda.gov/Hardzone/*. Find out what climate zone you live in.

☐ 5. Go to *http://www.garden.org/foodguide/browse*. Find out what kinds of plants can grow in your climate.

☐ 6. Decide how big you would like the garden to be. It should be no larger than a typical lot in the city would be. Outline the lot on graph paper. Write the perimeter and area of the lot on the paper.

☐ 7. Design your garden on the paper. Use colored pencils to shade it. Use your notes to make sure you are including everything you need.

☐ 8. Include measurements and the scale on your design.

☐ 9. Complete the assessment rubric.

Name _____ Date _____

Activity 1
WEB QUEST
Chapter 3

**Cities**

# Plan a Garden for an Inner-City Lot

## EVALUATION

| Math Skills | Point Value | My Score | FINAL SCORE |
|---|---|---|---|
| Find the perimeter and area of garden spaces. (Step 6) | 2 | | |
| Use measurement to plan a garden to scale. (Steps 6–8) | 3 | | |
| **Social Studies Skills** | **Point Value** | **My Score** | **FINAL SCORE** |
| Research climate in your area. (Steps 4 and 5) | 2 | | |
| Research information about community spaces. (Steps 1 and 2) | 3 | | |
| **Technology Skills** | **Point Value** | **My Score** | **FINAL SCORE** |
| Use the Internet to visit sites about community gardens. (Steps 1–3) | 2 | | |
| Find information about climate and gardens by navigating Web sites. (Steps 4 and 5) | 3 | | |

TOTAL SCORE _____

Teacher's Initials _____

## CONCLUSION

Answer the following questions on a separate sheet of paper.

1. Why do people create community gardens?
2. What was the perimeter and area of your garden?
3. Why is it necessary to plan all the details of a garden before creating one?

ACROSS THE CURRICULUM Math Connections

Activity 2

## Profiles in Math

Rachel Carson was a writer and a scientist who worked to protect the environment from harmful pesticides. After World War II, many farmers began using dangerous chemicals to control pests. In 1962, Carson wrote her book *Silent Spring* in which she described the damage these pesticides had done to animals and the environment. Because of her work, she is sometimes called "the mother of modern environmentalism."

# Research Natural Pest Control

## Objectives

**Math** To reinforce studies of measuring and graphing by creating a graph to illustrate a report

**Science** To reinforce studies of plants by researching natural pest-control methods

**Technology** To use a word processing program to write a report about pest control

**Bloom's Taxonomy** Applying and Evaluating

## Prerequisites

- Practice graphing data.
- Study types of pests that attack plants.
- Review the use of a word processing program.

## Additional Applications

**Social Studies** Agriculture

**Language Arts** Descriptive Language

**Scale UP** Have each student create a garden plan indicating where to plant companion plants.

**Scale BACK** Have students create graphs in small groups.

## Materials

copies of the "Plants: Research Natural Pest Control" Warm-Up and Directions, pp. 40 and 41 • computers with Internet access, word processing programs, and printers • graph paper • rulers • pencils • pens

**Alternate Materials:** science books and journals about insects

## Web Resources

- http://www.noahsnotes.com/naturalpest.html
- https://www.buglogical.com/catalog.asp?action=showCatalog&typeNumber=12&sectionNumber=25
- http://eartheasy.com/grow_garden_insectary.htm

**1.** Complete the **Warm-Up** activity on page 40. Review types of graphs, including how to plot points on a line graph. Review the needs and enemies of plants. Demonstrate how to use a word processing program.

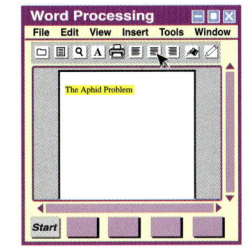

**2.** If computer access is not available, have students use science books and journals to find information and then write their reports by hand.

**3.** Distribute the **Directions** on page 41. Have students make a line graph showing the number of ladybugs needed to control a set number of aphids in a garden. Help any students who have trouble figuring out the setup of the line graph. Make sure they plot the number of ladybugs and the number of aphids along the two axes with the numbers of ladybugs increasing along the *x*-axis. Make sure the numbers increase by hundreds.

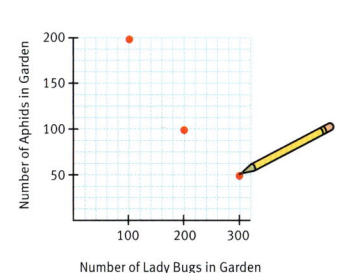

**4.** Help students print their reports, and have them present the reports to the class.

**5.** Complete the assessment rubric on page 41.

**Math Standard:** The student solves problems by collecting, organizing, displaying, and interpreting sets of data.
**Science Standard:** The student constructs simple graphs, tables, maps, and charts to organize, examine, and evaluate information.
**Technology Standard:** The student produces documents at the keyboard.
**Bloom's Taxonomy:** Applying—identify the relationship between ladybugs and aphids
Evaluating—judge formalized results on a graph

CHAPTER 3 Measuring and Graphing • Plants

39

Name _____ Date _____

Activity 2
Warm-Up
Chapter 3

**Plants**

# Research Natural Pest Control

### FOCUS

Completely fill in the bubble of the best answer for each item below.

**Math**
On a line graph, points are plotted using

Ⓐ bars.
Ⓑ pie charts.
Ⓒ *x* and *y* coordinates.
Ⓓ circles.

**Science**
Plants must have all of the following **EXCEPT**

Ⓕ sunlight.
Ⓖ rocks.
Ⓗ water.
Ⓙ nutrients.

**Technology**
To center text, you use the _____ button.

Ⓚ Align Center
Ⓛ Print
Ⓜ Align Left
Ⓝ Align Right

### PLAN

Imagine you have a small vegetable garden. You notice a problem. There is a strange, sticky goo on some plant stems. You have seen small green insects crawling on the plants. You decide to find information about them. Read about each garden pest, and circle the one you think is affecting your garden.

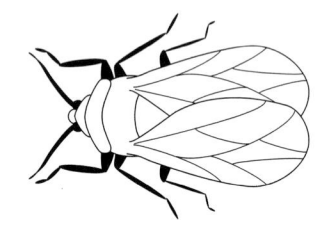

| | |
|---|---|
| Adult whiteflies are white insects with wings. | Two-spotted spider mites are difficult to see. |
| Aphids are pear-shaped and are often green. They produce a sticky substance called honeydew. | Slugs are oval-shaped and usually grey or brown. They leave a slimy trail. |

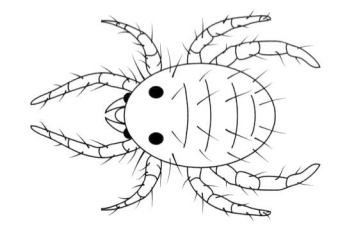

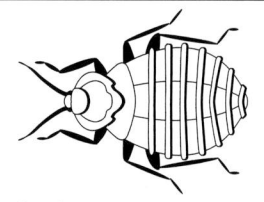

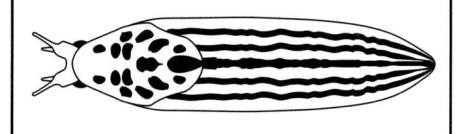

ACROSS THE CURRICULUM Math Connections

Name _____ Date _____

Activity 2
Directions
Chapter 3

**Plants**

# Research Natural Pest Control

**CREATE**

Follow these steps to research natural pest control.

☐ 1. Go to *http://www.noahsnotes.com/naturalpest.html*. Look for information about safe insect control.

☐ 2. Go to *https://www.buglogical.com/catalog.asp?action= showCatalog&typeNumber=12&sectionNumber=25*. Determine how many ladybugs you should order.

☐ 3. Go to *http://eartheasy.com/grow_garden_insectary.htm*. Decide on five types of plants you could grow to help keep ladybugs in your garden.

☐ 4. Open a new word processing document. Describe the problem from the **Warm-Up,** and describe your plan of attack over the next month. Give your report a title, make it boldface, and center it. Save and print your document.

☐ 5. Using graph paper, make a line graph to show the relationship between the number of aphids and the number of ladybugs in your garden. Present your plan to the class.

☐ 6. Complete the assessment rubric.

**CHECK**

| Math Skills | Point Value | My Score | FINAL SCORE |
|---|---|---|---|
| Create a line graph. (Step 5) | 5 | | |

| Science Skills | Point Value | My Score | FINAL SCORE |
|---|---|---|---|
| Research information about insects. (Steps 1–3) | 5 | | |

| Technology Skills | Point Value | My Score | FINAL SCORE |
|---|---|---|---|
| Create a word processing document. (Step 4) | 5 | | |

**TOTAL SCORE** _____

Teacher's Initials _____

ACROSS THE CURRICULUM Math Connections

**Activity 1**

## Profiles in Math

**T**imothy J. Pennings, a mathematician at Hope College, has discovered that dogs use math. He noticed that when playing catch with his dog Elvis, the dog always found the fastest angles and paths. By applying math equations to Elvis's paths, Pennings discovered the dog was solving a complicated math problem. "Elvis's behavior," Pennings says, "is an example of the uncanny way in which nature often finds optimal solutions."

Space ART

# Design a Dog Park

## Objectives

**Math** To reinforce studies of approximate measure by measuring for a dog-park design

**Fine Arts** To reinforce studies of the element of space by designing a dog park

**Technology** To use a drawing and graphics program to create a park design

**Bloom's Taxonomy** Remembering and Applying

## Prerequisites

- Practice using approximate measurement.
- Study the use of space in art.
- Review the use of the Shape tools in a drawing and graphics program.

## Additional Applications

**Science** Animals

**Social Studies** Community

**Scale UP** Have each student build a scale model of his or her park.

**Scale BACK** Have students incorporate only two features in their parks.

## Materials

copies of the "Space: Design a Dog Park" Warm-Up and Directions, pp. 44 and 45
- computers with Internet access, drawing and graphics programs, and printers • yardsticks

**Alternate Materials:** drawing paper • rulers
- markers

## Web Resources

- http://www.dogpark.com/
- http://www.inch.com/~dogs/runs.html
- http://home.earthlink.net/~ejlmp/dpd.html

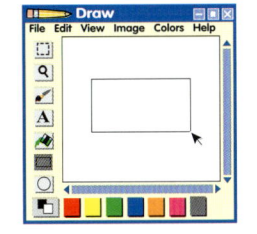

**1.** Complete the **Warm-Up** activity on page 44. Review using approximate measure, and remind students how to find area. Review positive and negative space in three-dimensional design and art. Demonstrate how to use the Shape, Fill, and Text Box tools in a drawing and graphics program.

**2.** If computer access is not available, have students use paper, rulers, and markers to create their designs.

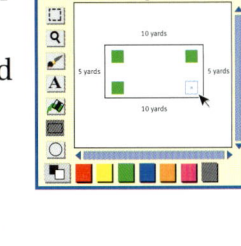

**3.** Distribute the **Directions** on page 45. The Web site in Step 1 is above level for students. Read aloud relevant information. Set aside time to take the class to a nearby park, and help them use yardsticks to find the approximate measures of the area. Make sure students have received parental permission before taking a field trip.

**4.** Help students print their designs, and have them share the designs with the class.

**5.** Complete the assessment rubric on page 45.

**Math Standard:** The student estimates and measures lengths using standard units such as inch, foot, yard, centimeter, decimeter, and meter.
**Fine Arts Standard:** The student develops a variety of effective compositions, using design skills.
**Technology Standard:** The student uses appropriate software to express ideas including the use of graphics.
**Bloom's Taxonomy:** Remembering—recall researched information on dog parks
Applying—use research in an original design

CHAPTER 4 Multiplication Concepts • Space

43

Name _____  Date _____

Activity 1
Warm-Up
Chapter 4

**Space**

# Design a Dog Park

> **FOCUS**
>
> Completely fill in the bubble of the best answer for each item below.
>
> **Math**
> There are 3 feet in a yard. If a park is about 4 yards long, then the park is **MORE** than
>
> Ⓐ 19 feet long.
> Ⓑ 15 feet long.
> Ⓒ 9 feet long.
> Ⓓ 24 feet long.
>
> **Fine Arts**
> Negative space is
>
> Ⓕ the empty area around an artwork.
> Ⓖ the unhappy feeling an artist has.
> Ⓗ the solid area of an artwork.
> Ⓙ the use of dark colors.
>
> **Technology**
> The **BEST** tool to use to make a rectangle in a drawing and graphics document would be
>
> Ⓚ the Paintbrush tool.
> Ⓛ the Rectangle Shape tool.
> Ⓜ the Line tool.
> Ⓝ the Text Box tool.

**PLAN**

1. Fill in the diagram below with specific ways dogs like to play.

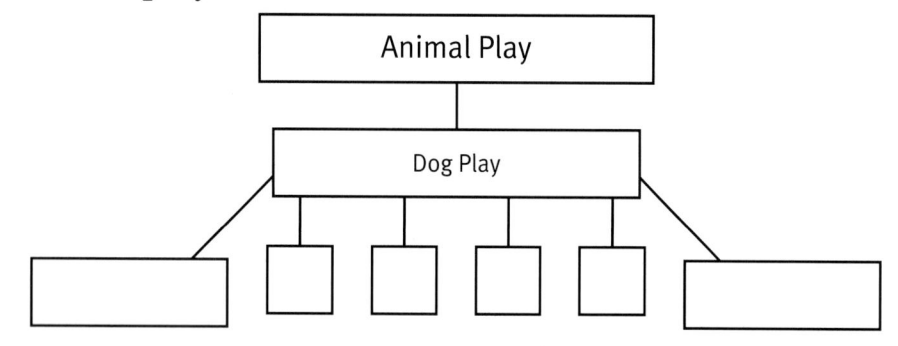

   ```
              Animal Play
                   |
               Dog Play
           /    |    |    |    \
         [ ]  [ ]  [ ]  [ ]  [ ]
   ```

2. On a separate sheet of paper, design and label a park area that relates to one of your ideas.

44  ACROSS THE CURRICULUM Math Connections

Name _____ Date _____

Activity 1

Directions

Chapter 4

**Space**

# Design a Dog Park

**CREATE**

Follow these steps to design a dog park.

☐ 1. Go to *http://www.dogpark.com/*. Click **Dog Parks,** and listen as your teacher reads the paragraph. Click **Dog Parks in the USA.** Take notes. Click **How To: Starting a Dog Park Resources.** Take notes.

☐ 2. Imagine your mayor has decided to change a nearby park into a dog park. Use a yardstick to find the park's approximate area.

☐ 3. Open a new drawing and graphics document. Use the Shape tools to draw the park area. Label the sides with their measurements.

☐ 4. Decide what items you need in your dog park and how to use space in your park. Create small squares to represent each item, and use color to distinguish various features. Save your design. Create a new drawing and graphics document. Make and save a symbol key.

☐ 5. Print your documents. Share them with the class.

☐ 6. Complete the assessment rubric.

**CHECK**

| Math Skills | Point Value | My Score | FINAL SCORE |
|---|---|---|---|
| Use approximate measurement. (Step 2) | 5 | | |
| **Fine Arts Skills** | **Point Value** | **My Score** | **FINAL SCORE** |
| Use space in an original park design. (Steps 3 and 4) | 5 | | |
| **Technology Skills** | **Point Value** | **My Score** | **FINAL SCORE** |
| Use the Shape tools. (Steps 3 and 4) | 5 | | |

TOTAL SCORE _____

Teacher's Initials _____

ACROSS THE CURRICULUM Math Connections

# Activity 2

## History of Math

**A** counting board was a tool used by ancient cultures as a mechanical aid for counting. A counting board consisted of a piece of wood, stone, or metal with carved grooves or painted lines. The person using the counting board moved beads, pebbles, or metal discs between the grooves to perform calculations. The oldest surviving counting board, called the *Salamis tablet,* was used by the Babylonians around 300 B.C.

**Informational Text**

LANGUAGE ARTS WebQuest

# Compare Types of Assistance Dogs

## Objectives

**Math** To reinforce studies of skip counting by skip counting to compare assistance dogs

**Language Arts** To reinforce studies of informational text by writing informational text about assistance dogs

**Technology** To use a presentation program to give a presentation

**Bloom's Taxonomy** Analyzing and Creating

## Prerequisites

- Practice skip counting using various numbers.
- Practice writing informational text.
- Review how to use a presentation program.

## Additional Applications

**Social Studies** Following or Giving Directions

**Science** Inherited Characteristics

**Scale UP** Have students prepare an informational handout to support their presentation.

**Scale BACK** Have students give a presentation about one type of assistance dog.

## Materials

copies of the "Informational Text: Compare Types of Assistance Dogs" WebQuest, pp. 48–51 • computers with Internet access, presentation programs, and printers • projector

**Alternate Materials:** MathTools **Number Line Tool**

## WebQuest Map

**Task:**
"Buying Blind," an article about being blind,
http://www.iaadp.org/buy_blind.html

**Process:**

STEP 1 http://www.assistancedog.org/industry_info/assistance_dog_roles.html

STEP 2 http://www.iaadp.org/tasks.html

STEP 3 http://www.adionline.org/

STEP 4 http://www.assistancedog.org/industry_info/etiquette.html

STEP 5 http://www.workingdogs.com/articles_serv.htm

**1.** Distribute the **WebQuest** on pages 48–51. Review skip counting. Discuss assistance dogs, and ask students to share what they know about assistance dogs such as guide dogs, hearing dogs, and service dogs. Review how to use a presentation program, and discuss how a presentation program can be used to give an informational presentation.

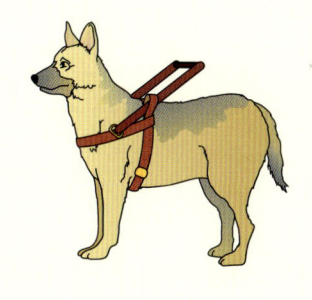

**2.** For the **Task,** locate the article "Buying Blind" online, and print or make copies for the class. Distribute the article, and discuss what it would be like to be blind and to go shopping with a guide dog.

**3.** Have students use a projector to give their presentations. If a projector is not available, have students give their presentations in small groups around the computer screen.

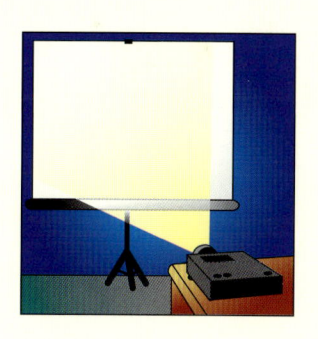

**4.** Complete the assessment rubric on page 51.

**Math Standard:** The student identifies patterns in multiplication facts using concrete objects, pictorial models, or technology.
**Language Arts Standard:** The student writes to communicate with a variety of audiences.
**Technology Standard:** The student uses presentation software to communicate with specific audiences.
**Bloom's Taxonomy:** Analyzing—compare types of assistance dogs
Creating—produce an informational presentation

**CHAPTER 4 Multiplication Concepts • Informational Text**

Name _____ Date _____

**Activity 2**

**WEB QUEST**
Chapter 4

**Informational Text**

# Compare Types of Assistance Dogs

### INTRODUCTION

Assistance dogs are dogs that are trained to increase the independence of people with disabilities, including those who have sensory and physical impairments. The first assistance dogs to be trained in the United States were guide dogs, which help people who are blind or visually impaired. Other types of assistance dogs include hearing dogs, which assist people who are deaf or hearing impaired, and service dogs, which aid people with physical disabilities. Social dogs are another type of assistance dog that work in animal-assisted therapy at hospitals, nursing homes, and other institutions, but are not recognized as "service animals" by U.S. law. You are going to research the different types of assistance dogs and write informational text for a presentation. You will use math to compare the types of assistance dogs.

Name _____  Date _____

Activity 2

**Informational Text**

# Compare Types of Assistance Dogs

WEB QUEST — Chapter 4

> **TASK**
>
> You are an informational speaker who is giving a presentation on assistance dogs to an elementary school. It is important that the students know what an assistance dog is and are able to recognize the different types of assistance dogs. Your job is to research assistance dogs and prepare a presentation comparing the types of assistance dogs.
>
> The specific question you have to consider is *What are the distinguishing characteristics of each type of assistance dog?*
>
> Before you begin your individual research, read the article "Buying Blind." Discuss the challenges involved in doing everyday tasks with a guide dog.

ACROSS THE CURRICULUM Math Connections

Name _____ Date _____ Activity 2

**WEB QUEST Chapter 4**

**Informational Text**

# Compare Types of Assistance Dogs

**PROCESS**

Follow these steps to compare types of assistance dogs.

☐ 1. Go to *http://www.assistancedog.org/industry_info/assistance_dog_roles.html* to read about assistance dog roles.

☐ 2. Go to *http://www.iaadp.org/tasks.html* to research assistance dog tasks. Take notes on the tasks each type of assistance dog performs. Skip count to quickly count the number of tasks listed for each type of dog. Compare the number of tasks each type of dog may need to learn.

☐ 3. Go to *http://www.adionline.org/*, and click the links to view training standards for service, hearing, guide, and social dogs. Research the number of hours and months of training required for each type of service dog. Skip count to calculate the number of hours required for guide-dog training. You can use the ***eMathTools: Number Line Tool.*** Compare the training of each type of service dog, and take notes.

☐ 4. Go to *http://www.assistancedog.org/industry_info/etiquette.html* to read about etiquette with assistance dogs.

☐ 5. Go to *http://www.workingdogs.com/articles_serv.htm*. Click the links to read articles about assistance dogs. Take notes.

☐ 6. Open a new presentation program. Create a title slide for your presentation, and write an introduction. Then create a title slide and informational slides for each type of assistance dog. Write a conclusion slide that compares the different types of assistance dogs. Preview your slide-show presentation.

☐ 7. Complete the assessment rubric.

ACROSS THE CURRICULUM Math Connections

Name _____ Date _____    Activity 2

**Informational Text**

WEB QUEST
Chapter 4

# Compare Types of Assistance Dogs

### EVALUATION

| Math Skills | Point Value | My Score | FINAL SCORE |
|---|---|---|---|
| Compare training time hours and months. (Step 3) | 2 | | |
| Use skip counting to solve problems. (Steps 2 and 3) | 3 | | |
| **Language Arts Skills** | Point Value | My Score | FINAL SCORE |
| Research information for a presentation. (Steps 1–5) | 2 | | |
| Write informational text. (Step 6) | 3 | | |
| **Technology Skills** | Point Value | My Score | FINAL SCORE |
| Enter a URL and view a Web page. (Steps 1–5) | 2 | | |
| Use a presentation program to create slides. (Step 6) | 3 | | |

TOTAL SCORE _____

Teacher's Initials _____

### CONCLUSION

Answer the following questions on a separate sheet of paper.

1. What did you learn about assistance dogs?
2. Why is it important to research information before giving a presentation?
3. How would you have completed this task without the aid of a presentation program?

ACROSS THE CURRICULUM Math Connections

### Activity 1

### History of Math

A scanner is a device that captures and converts images to a digital format. A scanner has an array of photosensitive cells that detect light reflected off or transmitted through the object being scanned. This array of receptors measures light intensity and converts it into an electrical charge. A scanner must have a light source, a light detector, converters to change brightness data into zeroes and ones for each pixel, and scanning software.

Goods
# SOCIAL STUDIES

# Edit Images of Appalachian Arts and Crafts

## Objectives

**Math** To reinforce studies of multiplying by 5 and 10 by resizing images

**Social Studies** To reinforce studies of goods by finding images of Appalachian arts and crafts

**Technology** To use a scanner and image editing software to scan and edit images

**Bloom's Taxonomy** Remembering and Applying

## Prerequisites

- Practice multiplying by 5 and 10.
- Study how community goods are bought and sold.
- Use gadgets such as a scanner.

## Additional Applications

**Language Arts** Descriptive Writing

**Science** Inherited and Learned Characteristics

**Scale UP** Have students create a slide show of Appalachian arts and crafts using a presentation program.

**Scale BACK** Have students work in pairs to capture and edit an image using explicit instructions.

## Materials

copies of the "Goods: Edit Images of Appalachian Arts and Crafts" Warm-Up and Directions, pp. 54 and 55 • computers with Internet access and image editing programs • scanner or digital camera • books about Appalachian arts and crafts • pencils • paper

## Web Resources

- http://portfolio.psu.edu/build/collect/multimedia3.html
- http://www.apptrav.com/folk.html

1. Have students complete the **Warm-Up** activity on page 54. Practice multiplying numbers by 5 and 10. Discuss how goods are bought and sold. Have students look at pictures of Appalachian arts and crafts on the Internet or in books.

2. Students can capture images from the Internet and save them according to your school's policy for saving files. They can also use a digital camera to capture images or use a scanner to capture pictures from books or photos. Check copyrights to ensure that reproduction is permitted for educational use.

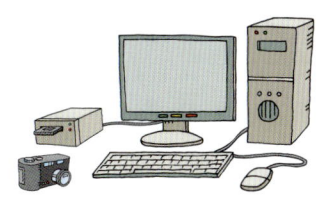

3. Distribute the **Directions** on page 55. Explain to students how to capture the images and where to save them. Show students how to use the image editing program, including how to adjust the size, crop an image, and work with tools and basic color.

4. For Steps 3 and 4, students should be able to view the image properties using one of the menus in the image editing program. They should be able to find the image dimensions as well as the size of the file. Increasing the image by 5 times (500%) will not necessarily increase the file size by 5 times. The overall area will be increased by 5 times, not each dimension.

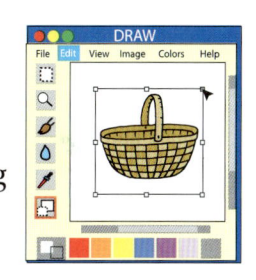

5. Complete the assessment rubric on page 55.

**Math Standard:** The student identifies patterns in multiplication facts.
**Social Studies Standard:** The student understands the concept of an economic system.
**Technology Standard:** The student uses a variety of input devices such as a scanner.
**Bloom's Taxonomy:** Remembering—recall information about how to use a scanner or image editing program
Applying—use knowledge of scanning and image editing to complete a project

CHAPTER 5 Multiplication and Division Facts • Goods   53

Name _____ Date _____

Activity 1
Warm-Up
Chapter 5

Goods

# Edit Images of Appalachian Arts and Crafts

## FOCUS

Completely fill in the bubble of the best answer for each item below.

**Math**
Which numbers are 5 and 10 times greater than 15?

- (A) 20 and 25
- (B) 75 and 150
- (C) 50 and 75
- (D) 25 and 100

**Social Studies**
Which is **NOT** an example of a good?

- (F) a box of cereal
- (G) a drum
- (H) a soccer ball
- (J) a sitting dog

**Technology**
Which would you **NOT** use an image editing program for?

- (K) making an image larger
- (L) taking a digital photo
- (M) changing the brightness of an image
- (N) cropping an image

## PLAN

1. Draw a picture of a finished artwork or craft.
2. Write the length and width on the drawing.
3. Write the measurements if you increased the size 5 times and then 10 times.

54

ACROSS THE CURRICULUM Math Connections

Name _____ Date _____ Activity 1

**Goods**

Directions
Chapter 5

# Edit Images of Appalachian Arts and Crafts

**CREATE**

Follow these steps to edit images of Appalachian arts and crafts.

- ☐ 1. Find images of Appalachian arts and crafts.
- ☐ 2. Capture an image using your computer software, digital camera, or scanner. Note the size of the image.
- ☐ 3. Make the image 5 times larger. Write down the size. Undo your resizing.
- ☐ 4. Make the image 10 times larger. Write down the size. Undo the resizing.
- ☐ 5. Crop the image. Adjust the color of the image. Save the image with a new name.
- ☐ 6. Repeat Steps 2–5 with other images.
- ☐ 7. Complete the assessment rubric.

**CHECK**

| Math Skills | Point Value | My Score | FINAL SCORE |
|---|---|---|---|
| Increase an image by 5 and 10 times. (Steps 3 and 4) | 5 | | |
| **Social Studies Skills** | **Point Value** | **My Score** | **FINAL SCORE** |
| Identify Appalachian arts and crafts. (Step 1) | 5 | | |
| **Technology Skills** | **Point Value** | **My Score** | **FINAL SCORE** |
| Capture and adjust an image. (Steps 2–5) | 5 | | |

TOTAL SCORE _____

Teacher's Initials _____

ACROSS THE CURRICULUM Math Connections

**Activity 2**

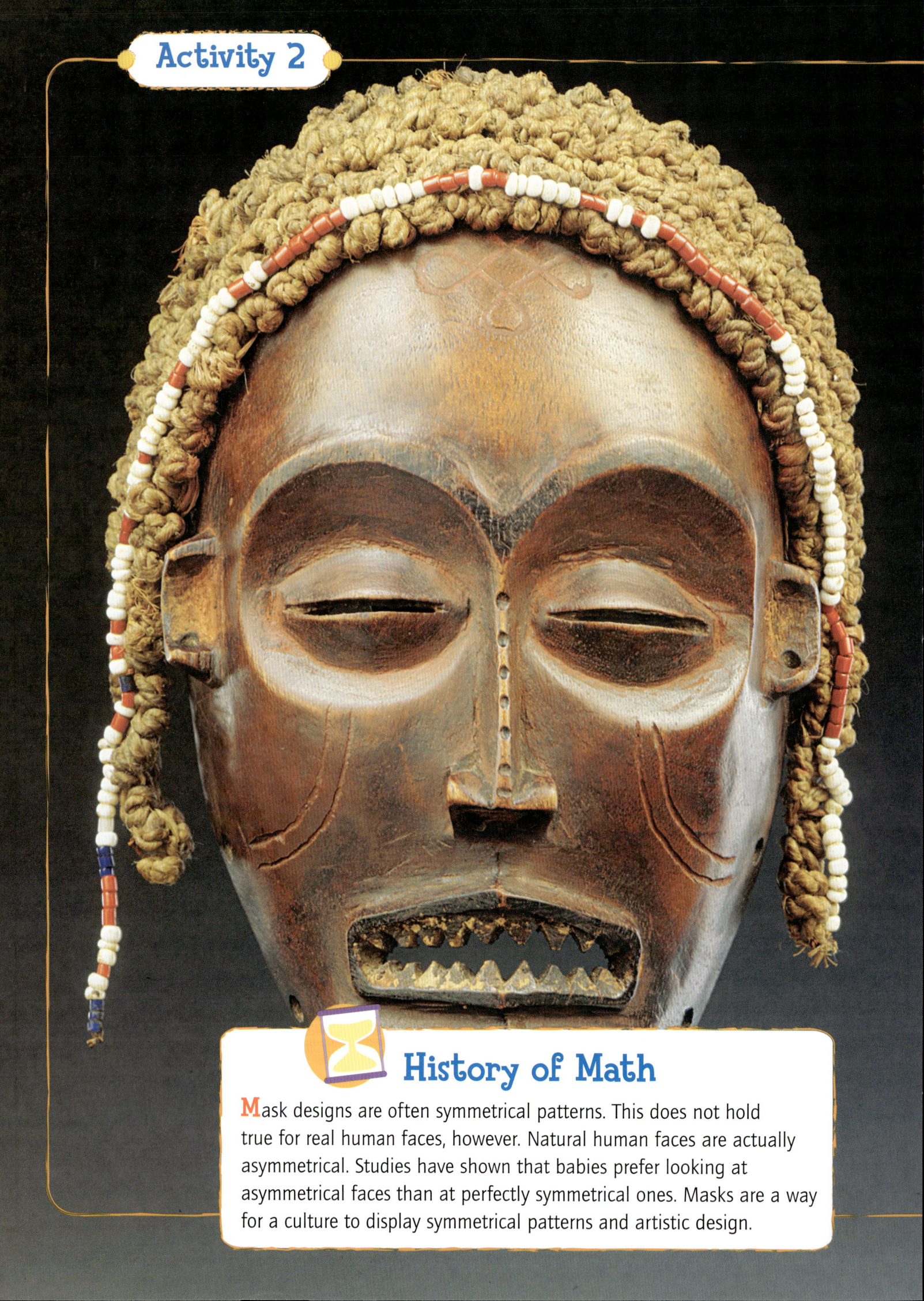

## History of Math

Mask designs are often symmetrical patterns. This does not hold true for real human faces, however. Natural human faces are actually asymmetrical. Studies have shown that babies prefer looking at asymmetrical faces than at perfectly symmetrical ones. Masks are a way for a culture to display symmetrical patterns and artistic design.

**Shape and Form**

# Create a Presentation about African Art

### Objectives

**Math** To reinforce studies of multiplication by multiplying facial features by 0, 1, and 2 to create a mask

**Fine Arts** To reinforce studies of form and shape by sculpting a three-dimensional mask

**Technology** To use a presentation program to create a presentation about African art

**Bloom's Taxonomy** Applying and Creating

### Prerequisites

- Practice multiplying numbers by 0, 1, and 2.
- Review the elements of form and shape.
- Review how to copy and paste images into a presentation program.

### Additional Applications

**Science** Environments
**Social Studies** World Cultures
**Scale UP** Have each group member create an individual mask.
**Scale BACK** Have students draw and paint masks.

### Materials

copies of the "Shape and Form: Create a Presentation about African Art" WebQuest, pp. 58–61 • computers with Internet access and presentation programs • butcher paper • masking tape • 9″ paper plates • air-dry modeling clay • petroleum jelly • plaster of paris strips • containers of water • paintbrushes • acrylic paints

### WebQuest Map

**Task:**
"Playful Performers," Web site with background on masks in African society,
http://www.nmafa.si.edu/exhibits/playful/introindex.html

**Process:**
STEP 1 http://www.kidsart.com/IS/401.html
STEP 2 http://www.arttribal.com/ALLMASKS/index.htm
STEP 3 http://www.guruve.com/gallery/index.html

**1.** Distribute the **WebQuest** on pages 58–61. Review multiplication facts for 0, 1, and 2. Choose an example of a form, and have students identify the types of space and shape present in and around it. Demonstrate how to copy a digital image. Demonstrate pasting an image into a Title and Content slide in a presentation program.

**2.** Find the Web site "Playful Performers." Have students discuss the use of different types of masks.

**3.** Divide students into groups. For Step 5 of the **WebQuest**, use masking tape to attach butcher paper to the working areas, and distribute the materials.

**4.** Students may need help using the plaster of paris strips. Make sure students crisscross the strips to form at least three layers. Help them remove the dry mask very gently.

**5.** Have students share their presentations and masks with the class.

**6.** Complete the assessment rubric on page 61.

**Math Standard:** The student solves and records multiplication problems (one-digit multiplier).
**Fine Arts Standard:** The student compares content in artwork from the past and present for various purposes such as telling stories and documenting history and traditions.
**Technology Standard:** The student uses graphics to ensure that products are appropriate for the communication media including multimedia screen displays.
**Bloom's Taxonomy:** Applying—use research on masks in a mask design
Creating—create a mask and a presentation about African art

CHAPTER 5 Multiplication and Division Facts • Shape and Form

Name _____ Date _____

**Activity 2**

**Shape and Form**

# Create a Presentation about African Art

### INTRODUCTION

Masks have been used in Africa for thousands of years. They were used in important dance ceremonies and festivals. Traditional African artwork influenced artists such as Picasso and continues to influence contemporary artists around the world. Many African artists today allow traditional art to influence their creations. You will research traditional African masks and create a mask inspired by them.

Name _____ Date _____

**Activity 2**

**WEB QUEST**

**Chapter 5**

**Shape and Form**

# Create a Presentation about African Art

**TASK**

You are a member of a group of artists. Your group is interested in how traditional art forms influence artists today. You want to create a mask inspired by traditional African masks. You will first research African masks and compare them with contemporary African art. You will create a nonrealistic facial mask inspired by these masks. You will then create a presentation comparing traditional masks with your design.

The specific question you have to consider is *How are modern artists inspired by traditional art forms?*

Before you begin your research, listen as your teacher reads sections from the Web site "Playful Performers." Discuss the role of traditional masks in different African cultures.

ACROSS THE CURRICULUM Math Connections

Name _____ Date _____

**Activity 2**
**WEB QUEST**
**Chapter 5**

## Shape and Form

# Create a Presentation about African Art

**PROCESS**

Follow these steps to create a presentation about African art.

☐ 1. Go to *http://www.kidsart.com/IS/401.html*. Read about African masks.

☐ 2. Go to *http://www.arttribal.com/ALLMASKS/index.htm*. Click different masks. Notice nonrealistic facial features.

☐ 3. Go to *http://www.guruve.com/gallery/index.html*. Click **list artists,** and then click names of African artists. Read about them, and look at their work.

☐ 4. In your group, discuss and choose four masks from your research.

☐ 5. With your group, apply clay to a paper plate, and sculpt it to form a mask. In your design, multiply one facial feature by 0, one by 1, and one by 2 to create a nonrealistic face. Include details inspired by the masks you chose. Let dry.

☐ 6. Apply a thin coat of petroleum jelly to the mask. Dip plaster of paris strips into water, and layer them across the clay, crisscrossing several times. Let dry.

☐ 7. Carefully take the paper mask off the clay. Paint it.

☐ 8. Open a new presentation. Go to the Web sites, copy the image of each mask you chose, and paste it onto a new Title and Content slide in your presentation. Title the mask, and add a sentence explaining what details inspired your group mask. Save your presentation.

☐ 9. Share your presentation and mask with the class.

☐ 10. Complete the assessment rubric.

ACROSS THE CURRICULUM Math Connections

Name _____ Date _____  Activity 2

**Shape and Form**

WEB QUEST
Chapter 5

# Create a Presentation about African Art

## EVALUATION

| Math Skills | Point Value | My Score | FINAL SCORE |
|---|---|---|---|
| Use numbers to create a mask design. (Step 5) | 1 | | |
| Multiply numbers by 0, 1, and 2. (Step 5) | 4 | | |
| **Fine Arts Skills** | **Point Value** | **My Score** | **FINAL SCORE** |
| Compare contemporary and traditional African art. (Step 3) | 2 | | |
| Create a mask inspired by traditional African masks. (Steps 5 and 6) | 3 | | |
| **Technology Skills** | **Point Value** | **My Score** | **FINAL SCORE** |
| Enter a URL and view a Web page. (Steps 1–3) | 2 | | |
| Copy and paste images into a presentation. (Step 8) | 3 | | |

**TOTAL SCORE** _____
Teacher's Initials _____

## CONCLUSION

Answer the following questions on a separate sheet of paper.
1. What facial features did you change through multiplication for your mask design?
2. Which traditional mask was your favorite? Why?

ACROSS THE CURRICULUM Math Connections

**Activity 1**

## Careers in Math

**D**rafters create drawings that show the dimensions, materials, procedures, and structures related to a building or a machine design. Drafters used to create these drawings by hand using rulers, protractors, and pencils, but most modern drafters now use special computer programs to create their designs. Drafters take general designs made by architects or engineers and create technical drawings that are very specific.

**Simple Machines**

SCIENCE WebQuest

# Design Playground Equipment

## Objectives

**Math** To reinforce studies of functions by writing and solving a function related to playground design

**Science** To reinforce studies of simple machines by creating playground equipment that uses simple machines

**Technology** To use a drawing and graphics program to design playground equipment

**Bloom's Taxonomy** Applying and Creating

## Prerequisites

- Practice writing and solving simple functions.
- Review types of simple machines.
- Review how to use the Line and Pencil tools in a drawing and graphics program.

## Additional Applications

**Language Arts** Explaining a Process

**Fine Arts** Line

**Scale UP** Have each group create a three-dimensional model of one piece of equipment.

**Scale BACK** Have each group create designs for only three pieces of equipment.

## Materials

copies of the "Simple Machines: Design Playground Equipment" WebQuest, pp. 64–67
• computers with Internet access and drawing and graphics programs • drawing paper • pencils • rulers

**Alternate Materials:** eMathTools *Function Machine*

## WebQuest Map

**Task:**
"Playground Pages: Let Kids Add Fun to Your Design," http://www.ptotoday.com/0803playground.html

**Process:**
STEP 1 http://cpsc.gov/cpscpub/pubs/327.html
STEP 2 http://www.bigtoys.com/products/catalog/5to12.asp
STEP 3 http://oac.schools.sa.edu.au/eshop/machine/index.html
STEP 4 http://library.thinkquest.org/CR0214980/

**1.** Distribute the **WebQuest** on pages 64–67. Review simple functions, and have students solve some functions. Have students identify examples of simple machines around the classroom. Demonstrate how to use the Line tool to make straight lines and the Pencil tool to make curved lines in a drawing and graphics program.

**2.** Find the online article "Playground Pages: Let Kids Add Fun to Your Design." Read it aloud, and have students discuss ways they can be involved in the playground design.

**3.** Divide students into small groups. Distribute the materials.

**4.** Some students may have trouble translating the problem in the **Task** into a function. The correct function should be $35 \rightarrow \div 7 \rightarrow n$, where the average number of students is the input (35) and the rule is ($\div 7$). Students should determine $n = 5$ in Step 5 of the **WebQuest.**

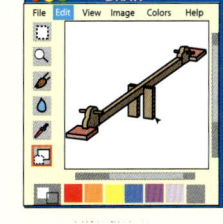

**5.** Complete the assessment rubric on page 67.

**Math Standard:** The student relates informal language to mathematical language and symbols.
**Science Standard:** The student observes a simple system and describes the role of various parts such as a yo-yo and string.
**Technology Standard:** The student uses appropriate software to express ideas including the use of multimedia.
**Bloom's Taxonomy:** Applying—use research about simple machines in playground equipment design
Creating—combine ideas about simple machines, drafting procedures, and the interests of children in playground equipment design

**CHAPTER 6 Functions • Simple Machines**

63

Name _____ Date _____

**Simple Machines**

# Design Playground Equipment

### INTRODUCTION

By the beginning of the 1900s, people in America had changed their view of children. Children were now protected from having to work, and more and more they were encouraged to go to school at an early age. People realized that children in big cities needed safe places to play in order to learn and grow, and they began to build playgrounds for these children. New Jersey and Virginia became the first states to create playground commissions and laws. This new idea that children needed to play in order to learn became more and more popular across the country. You are going to research modern playground design and create drafts for educational playground equipment to be built at a science museum.

Name _____ Date _____

Activity 1

**Simple Machines**

# Design Playground Equipment

**TASK**

You work for a playground equipment design company that is famous for its creativity. A science museum director has contacted you. The museum director wants to build a fun playground that teaches children about the three basic types of simple machines. In a normal hour on a normal day, an average of 35 children are at the museum. The director wants to make sure that there is one piece of equipment for every 7 children in that group of 35. You will first refresh your knowledge of playground equipment design, and then research simple machines and types of drafting drawings. You will then design enough pieces of playground equipment for the average number of children visiting the museum.

The specific question you have to consider is *How can playground equipment teach children about simple machines in a fun way?*

Before you begin your research, listen as your teacher reads the article "Playground Pages: Let Kids Add Fun to Your Design." Discuss ideas you have for playgrounds you use.

ACROSS THE CURRICULUM Math Connections

**Name** _____ **Date** _____

Activity 1
WEB QUEST
Chapter 6

**Simple Machines**

# Design Playground Equipment

**PROCESS**

Follow these steps to design playground equipment.

☐ 1. Go to *http://cpsc.gov/cpscpub/pubs/327.html,* and read the article. Write down what design and safety issues are involved when creating playground equipment.

☐ 2. Go to *http://www.bigtoys.com/products/catalog/5to12.asp,* and click the drawings to see examples of creative playground equipment design. Take notes.

☐ 3. Go to *http://oac.schools.sa.edu.au/eshop/machine/index.html.* Click **Pulleys, Wheels,** and **Levers** to learn more about these simple machines.

☐ 4. Go to *http://library.thinkquest.org/CR0214980/,* and read about drafting. Click **Oblique** and **Isometric** to see examples of these types of drawings.

☐ 5. Brainstorm ideas for your playground equipment. Draw some sketches, and create one piece of equipment to illustrate each simple machine. Write the function described in the **Task** using arrow notation. Solve the function with the given input. You can use the *eMathTools: Function Machine.*

☐ 6. Open a new drawing and graphics document. Using the Line and Pencil tools, draft an oblique or isometric drawing for one piece of equipment. Open a new document, and repeat for each piece of equipment until all equipment has been drawn. Use the Text Box tool to label your drawings, and save them.

☐ 7. Share your drawings with the class.

☐ 8. Complete the assessment rubric.

ACROSS THE CURRICULUM Math Connections

Name _____ Date _____

Activity 1
WEB QUEST
Chapter 6

**Simple Machines**

# Design Playground Equipment

## EVALUATION

| Math Skills | Point Value | My Score | FINAL SCORE |
|---|---|---|---|
| Write a function in arrow notation. (Step 5) | 2 | | |
| Solve a function related to playground equipment. (Step 5) | 3 | | |
| **Science Skills** | **Point Value** | **My Score** | **FINAL SCORE** |
| Research simple machines. (Step 3) | 1 | | |
| Use simple machines in playground equipment design. (Steps 5 and 6) | 4 | | |
| **Technology Skills** | **Point Value** | **My Score** | **FINAL SCORE** |
| Enter a URL and view a Web page. (Steps 1-4) | 1 | | |
| Use the Line and Pencil tools in a drawing and graphics document. (Step 6) | 4 | | |

**TOTAL SCORE** _____

Teacher's Initials _____

## CONCLUSION

Answer the following questions on a separate sheet of paper.

1. What process did you use to write the function?
2. Which piece of equipment would be the most fun for children? Why?
3. Would you like to have a job drafting designs? Why or why not?

ACROSS THE CURRICULUM Math Connections

## Activity 2

### Profiles in Math

Around the third century B.C., the Greek mathematician Diophantus wrote the *Arithmetica*, a work on the solutions of algebraic equations and number theory. Of the thirteen original books, only six survive today, but they include the earliest record of using symbols to represent unknown quantities. In the *Arithmetica*, Diophantus considers the solutions of both linear and quadratic equations, but he considers only positive rational solutions.

# Write about a Fantasy Playground

### Objectives

**Math** To reinforce studies of functions by using functions to plan a fantasy playground

**Language Arts** To reinforce studies of fantasy by writing about a fantasy playground

**Technology** To use keyboarding skills to key a document

**Bloom's Taxonomy** Applying and Creating

### Prerequisites

- Practice applying functions to real-life situations.
- Read examples of fantasy, and practice writing fantasy.
- Review keyboarding skills.

### Additional Applications

**Science** Simple Machines
**Fine Arts** Shape
**Scale UP** Have students research playground equipment and create a budget to build their playground.
**Scale BACK** Write out the functions and rules for the playground, and have students only calculate the numbers.

### Materials

copies of the "Fantasy: Write about a Fantasy Playground" Warm-Up and Directions, pp. 70 and 71
- computers with word processing programs and printers • paper • pencils

### Web Resources

- http://score.kings.k12.ca.us/lessons/functions/machine.html
- http://216.119.115.23/fg/phrase2.cfm

**1.** Complete the **Warm-Up** activity on page 70. Review functions, and discuss situations in which students could use functions. Review fantasy, and discuss how fantasy writing is different from other genres. Review keyboarding skills such as proper finger reaches.

**2.** Distribute the **Directions** on page 71. Have students use functions to create rules for a playground. Have students exchange rules with another student and plan their playgrounds based on their new rules. Have students revise their drawings from the **Warm-Up.**

**3.** Students may have difficulty writing functions and rules for their playgrounds. Students should write functions using words to describe the relationship between items on their playground, such as *For every slide on the playground, there are two swings.* Students should write their functions using arrow notation, such as $x \rightarrow \times 2 \rightarrow y$, where $x$ is the number of slides and $y$ is the number of swings.

**4.** Have students write a description of their playground using a word processing program. Check students' keyboarding skills as they type. If computer access is not available, have students write their descriptions on paper.

**5.** Complete the assessment rubric on page 71.

**Math Standard:** The student applies mathematics to solve problems connected to everyday experiences and activities in and out of school.
**Language Arts Standard:** The student distinguishes fiction from nonfiction, including fact and fantasy.
**Technology Standard:** The student produces documents at the keyboard.
**Bloom's Taxonomy:** Applying—use functions to plan a playground
Creating—plan a fantasy playground

CHAPTER 6 Functions • Fantasy

Name _____ Date _____

Activity 2
Warm-Up
Chapter 6

**Fantasy**

# Write about a Fantasy Playground

**FOCUS**

Completely fill in the bubble of the best answer for each item below.

**Math**
The parts of a function are the

- Ⓐ variable and constant.
- Ⓑ rule and order.
- Ⓒ input, rule, and output.
- Ⓓ $x$ and $y$ coordinates.

**Language Arts**
Fantasy is a form of

- Ⓕ nonfiction.
- Ⓖ biography.
- Ⓗ periodical.
- Ⓙ fiction.

**Technology**
To type quickly on a keyboard, you need to

- Ⓚ use the Shift key.
- Ⓛ learn the proper finger reaches.
- Ⓜ use the mouse.
- Ⓝ sit close to the monitor.

**PLAN**

1. On a sheet of paper, write down what it would be like to have your own fantasy playground. Write down what real-life and what made-up things you would have in your playground.

2. On a separate piece of paper, draw a plan for your fantasy playground in pencil.

ACROSS THE CURRICULUM Math Connections

Name _____ Date _____

Activity 2

Directions

Chapter 6

**Fantasy**

# Write about a Fantasy Playground

## CREATE

Follow these steps to write about a fantasy playground.

☐ 1. Write a rule for the number of swings on a playground, such as *For every slide on the playground, there are two swings.* Write your rule as a function using arrow notation:
$x \rightarrow \times 2 \rightarrow y$.

☐ 2. Repeat Step 1 to create a set of rules for the number of items on a playground.

☐ 3. Exchange rules with another student. Use the new set of rules to calculate the number of each item for your playground.

☐ 4. Change your drawing from the **Warm-Up** to match the new rules.

☐ 5. Open a new word processing program. Use keyboarding skills to write a description of your fantasy playground.

☐ 6. Print your document.

☐ 7. Complete the assessment rubric.

## CHECK

| Math Skills | Point Value | My Score | FINAL SCORE |
|---|---|---|---|
| Write and solve functions that apply to real-life situations. (Steps 1–3) | 5 | | |
| **Language Arts Skills** | **Point Value** | **My Score** | **FINAL SCORE** |
| Write a description of a fantasy playground. (Step 5) | 5 | | |
| **Technology Skills** | **Point Value** | **My Score** | **FINAL SCORE** |
| Use keyboarding skills to produce documents at the keyboard. (Step 5) | 5 | | |

TOTAL SCORE _____

Teacher's Initials _____

ACROSS THE CURRICULUM Math Connections

# Activity 1

## History of Math

In the sixteenth century, a Bohemian count began minting coins from silver deposits. His coins were of such high quality that his *thalers*, named after the Joachimsthal valley, became famous around the world. Variants of the word *thaler* became the names of coins in many countries, including *dollar* in Scotland. The *dollar* is currently the name of the official currency of several countries, including the United States.

Economics

SOCIAL STUDIES WebQuest

# Create a Monetary System

## Objectives

**Math** To reinforce studies of multiplication by multiplying numbers by 10, 100, and 1,000 to create a monetary system

**Social Studies** To reinforce studies of economics by researching currency

**Technology** To use a spreadsheet program to organize and calculate data

**Bloom's Taxonomy** Understanding and Applying

## Prerequisites

- Practice multiplying numbers by 10, 100, and 1,000.
- Study the idea of currency as the basis for a monetary system.
- Review how to use a spreadsheet program.

## Additional Applications

**Language Arts** Visual Aids

**Science** Minerals

**Scale UP** Have students consider more complex ideas associated with a monetary system, such as how much money to issue, exchange rates, and standards.

**Scale BACK** Have students only create a design for the main unit of currency and base their system on the United States system.

## Materials

copies of the "Economics: Create a Monetary System" WebQuest, pp. 74–77 • computers with Internet access and spreadsheet programs • paper • pencils • rulers • colored pencils or crayons

**Alternate Materials:** eMathTools **Spreadsheet Tool**

### WebQuest Map

**Task:**
Web site about the history of money,
http://www.pbs.org/newshour/on2/money/history.html

**Process:**

STEP 2 http://fx.sauder.ubc.ca/currency_table.html

STEP 3 http://www.treas.gov/education/faq/currency/denominations.shtml

STEP 4 http://www.banknotes.com/images.htm
http://www.collectpapermoney.com/banknte.html

**1.** Distribute the **WebQuest** on pages 74–77. Practice multiplying numbers by 10, 100, and 1,000. Study the idea of currency, and discuss how it is a basis for a monetary system.

**2.** Encourage students to be creative when they create their names and designs. Have them make up a symbol ($, €, £, ¥) for the currency as well.

**3.** For Steps 2 and 3 of the **WebQuest,** give students more examples of currencies from other countries. If possible, bring in actual paper money or coins to help demonstrate. Explain that not all countries name their coins.

**4.** For Step 6, students should enter multiplication formulas to show how many of each subdivision is in the larger denomination. For example, in a spreadsheet, the formula $=B5*100$ under penny and next to $20.00 would result in 2,000, or 2,000 pennies. Only the first row of formulas needs to be filled in, as the **Fill Down** command can be used for the other rows. To use the **Fill Down** command, copy the cell, and click and drag within the column to fill in the remaining rows.

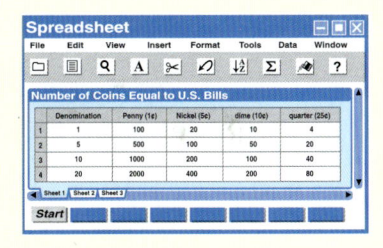

**5.** Complete the assessment rubric on page 77.

**Math Standard:** The student identifies patterns in related multiplication and division sentences.
**Social Studies Standard:** The student understands the concept of an economic system.
**Technology Standard:** The student uses appropriate software to solve problems including the use of spreadsheets.
**Bloom's Taxonomy:** Understanding—generalize ideas about currency by studying currencies of the world
Applying—use knowledge of monetary systems to create a new system

CHAPTER 7 Multidigit Multiplication and Division • Economics

Name _____ Date _____

**Activity 1**
**WEB QUEST**
**Chapter 7**

## Economics

# Create a Monetary System

### INTRODUCTION

Money is used around the world to buy goods and services. It is called the "medium of exchange." Money can be anything from shells, to beads, to oxen or other animals, to coins. Currency is the actual unit or form for exchange. Currency is dollars, euros, pesos, or pounds. Money as a medium of exchange is convenient for trade because it allows for a period of time between selling and buying goods and services. People don't exchange goods and services directly. Countries have their own currencies which differ in value and appearance from those of other countries. Images on coins and paper money often reflect historical events, national animals, heroes or heroines, and national pride. You are going to research the currencies and monetary systems of other countries and design your own monetary system and currency.

74   ACROSS THE CURRICULUM Math Connections

Name _____ Date _____

Activity 1

**Economics**

# Create a Monetary System

> **TASK**
>
> You have just discovered that a brand new country has been developed. The area that was once considered an island without a name has now become a new country, and its new government has appointed you as the new treasurer. The country needs a monetary system, or people won't be able to trade goods and services. It is up to you to decide what kind of currency will be created. It is also your task to design the bills and coins used.
>
> The specific questions you have to consider are *What will the units of currency be, and how will they be designed?*
>
> Before you begin your individual research, go to *http://www.pbs.org/newshour/on2/money/history.html,* and read some basic information about the history of money.

ACROSS THE CURRICULUM Math Connections

Name _____ Date _____   Activity 1

**Economics**

# Create a Monetary System

## PROCESS

Follow these steps to create a monetary system for a new country.

☐ 1. Select a name for the new country. Then select a name for the currency for the country. For example, the *dollar* is the main unit of currency of the United States. Decide what the format of the unit will be, such as paper or coin.

☐ 2. Create parts of your main unit. For example, the penny, nickel, dime, and quarter are all parts of the dollar. A penny is one cent, or $\frac{1}{100}$ of a dollar. Not all countries name their coins. Use the decimal system to create your parts. Go to *http://fx.sauder.ubc.ca/currency_table.html* to view the names of other countries' currencies.

☐ 3. Decide the multiples of your main unit. For example, the United States has a one-, two-, five-, ten-, twenty-, fifty-, and one hundred-dollar bill. Go to *http://www.treas.gov/education/faq/currency/denominations.shtml* to read more about denominations.

☐ 4. Design your currency. Go to *http://www.banknotes.com/images.htm* to view historical images of world paper money. Use a meaningful design for your currency. Go to *http://www.collectpapermoney.com/banknte.html* for explanations of the parts of a bank note. Draw your main unit of currency and any other denominations of the currency.

☐ 5. Make a spreadsheet to show your currency. Enter the names or values of your denominations and parts. You can use the **eMathTools: Spreadsheet Tool.**

☐ 6. Enter formulas that calculate the number of smaller units of your currency in the larger denominations.

☐ 7. Complete the assessment rubric.

Name _____ Date _____

Activity 1

**Economics**

# Create a Monetary System

## EVALUATION

| Math Skills | Point Value | My Score | FINAL SCORE |
|---|---|---|---|
| Use multiplication to solve problems. (Step 6) | 2 | | |
| Use multiplication and division to create a monetary system using the decimal system. (Steps 2 and 3) | 3 | | |
| **Social Studies Skills** | **Point Value** | **My Score** | **FINAL SCORE** |
| Research currencies of other countries. (Steps 2 and 4) | 2 | | |
| Create a new monetary system for a country. (Steps 1-4) | 3 | | |
| **Technology Skills** | **Point Value** | **My Score** | **FINAL SCORE** |
| Enter data into a spreadsheet. (Step 5) | 2 | | |
| Enter formulas into a spreadsheet. (Step 6) | 3 | | |

TOTAL SCORE _____

Teacher's Initials _____

## CONCLUSION

Answer the following questions on a separate sheet of paper.
1. How did you use multiplication to create your monetary system?
2. Does basing a monetary system on the decimal system make the use of currency simpler? Why or why not?

ACROSS THE CURRICULUM Math Connections

77

# Activity 2

## History of Math

**M**oney today is usually in the form of paper notes or metal coins, but that was not always the case. At different periods in history, shells were used in both China and Africa as money. China also used pieces of leather as money for a time. According to an ancient Greek historian, the first true coins were produced in Lydia, a country that was in what is now northwest Turkey.

**Physical Change**   SCIENCE

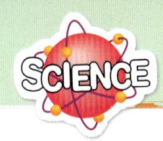

# Research Coin Minting

## Objectives

**Math** To reinforce studies of multiplication by applying multiplication to research on coin minting

**Science** To reinforce studies of physical change by learning about coin minting

**Technology** To use the Internet to research coin minting

**Bloom's Taxonomy** Remembering and Analyzing

## Prerequisites

- Practice applying multiplication to real-life situations.
- Study physical change.
- Review how to use an Internet search engine.

## Additional Applications

**Social Studies** Economics
**Fine Arts** Design
**Scale UP** Have students key and print their reports using a word processing program.
**Scale BACK** Have students write a series of facts based upon their research.

## Materials

copies of the "Physical Change: Research Coin Minting" Warm-Up and Directions, pp. 80 and 81
- computers with Internet access • writing paper
- pencils • colored pencils • pens

**Alternate Materials:** print research resources such as encyclopedias

## Web Resources

- http://www.usmint.gov/kids/index.cfm?fileContents=coinnews/preshow.cfm
- http://www.usmint.gov/kids
- http://www.treas.gov/education/
- http://www.ancienthistory.com/

**1.** Complete the **Warm-Up** activity on page 80. Practice applying multiplication to real-life situations. Review properties of matter and physical change. Demonstrate how to use an Internet search engine. If computer access is not available, have students perform research using print resources, such as encyclopedias.

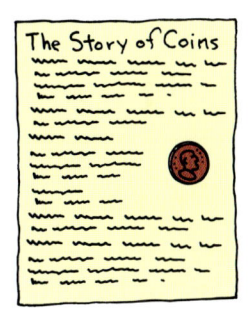

**2.** Distribute the **Directions** on page 81. Remind students to use decimals when multiplying coin amounts. Make sure that students evaluate Web sites for their appropriateness and accuracy when doing Internet research.

**3.** Have students present their reports to the class.

**4.** Complete the assessment rubric on page 81.

**Math Standard:** The student recognizes and solves problems in multiplication and division situations.
**Science Standard:** The student knows that matter has physical properties.
**Technology Standard:** The student applies appropriate electronic search strategies in the acquisition of information including key word search strategies.
**Bloom's Taxonomy:** Remembering—take notes to help recall research information
Analyzing—organize information into a research report

**CHAPTER 7 Multidigit Multiplication and Division • Physical Change**   79

Name _____  Date _____

**Activity 2**

**Warm-Up**

**Chapter 7**

## Physical Change

# Research Coin Minting

### FOCUS

Completely fill in the bubble of the best answer for each item below.

**Math**
If Jeremy has twenty quarters, what is the total amount of money that he has?

- Ⓐ $3.25
- Ⓑ $7.00
- Ⓒ $4.50
- Ⓓ $5.00

**Science**
If a metal is heated until it becomes a liquid, it has had

- Ⓕ a chemical change.
- Ⓖ a natural change.
- Ⓗ a physical change.
- Ⓙ no change.

**Technology**
To search for information about the history of coins,

- Ⓚ highlight the Search window.
- Ⓛ key the word *Search* in the search window.
- Ⓜ click the Search button.
- Ⓝ key the words *history* and *coins* in the Search window, and click the Search button.

### PLAN

1. Imagine you are going to design a new U.S. coin. On a separate sheet of paper, write what amount it would be for and what material you would make it out of.
2. Draw a series of pictures showing the way you could make your coin.

80  ACROSS THE CURRICULUM Math Connections

Name _____ Date _____

Activity 2

**Physical Change**

Directions

Chapter 7

# Research Coin Minting

**CREATE**

Follow these steps to research coin minting.

☐ 1. Go to *http://www.usmint.gov/kids/index.cfm?fileContents=coinnews/preshow.cfm*. View the show.

☐ 2. Go back to the Web site, click **Camp Coin,** and select **Coin Collector's Workshop.** Click and read **Ten Facts Every Coin Kid Should Know,** and find out how many coins the Mint makes each year. Multiply to find out about how many coins the Mint has produced since the year 2000.

☐ 3. Search for the U.S. Treasury's education site for students. Explore for information about coins. Take notes.

☐ 4. Perform a new search to find out about the history of coins. Take notes about materials used to make coins.

☐ 5. Choose an American coin, and using your notes, write a rough draft for a short report about the history of coins as if it is being told from this coin's point of view. Create illustrations for your paper.

☐ 6. Complete the assessment rubric.

**CHECK**

| Math Skills | Point Value | My Score | FINAL SCORE |
|---|---|---|---|
| Apply multiplication to the process of coin minting. (Step 2) | 5 | | |
| **Science Skills** | **Point Value** | **My Score** | **FINAL SCORE** |
| Research the physical change of metal to coins. (Steps 1–4) | 5 | | |
| **Technology Skills** | **Point Value** | **My Score** | **FINAL SCORE** |
| Perform a search using an Internet search engine. (Steps 3 and 4) | 5 | | |

TOTAL SCORE _____

Teacher's Initials _____

ACROSS THE CURRICULUM Math Connections

## Activity 1

### Careers in Math

For many years, food companies were allowed to say anything they wanted about their products in advertisements. That changed when the Center for Science in the Public Interest (CSPI), a group of scientists interested in the science of health, began to investigate food advertising. In the early 1990s, CSPI's efforts caused the government to make new laws about food packaging and advertisements.

Emphasis ART

# Create an Advertisement

### Objectives

**Math** To reinforce studies of fractions by finding and using a fraction in a product design

**Fine Arts** To use the principle of emphasis in a product design and advertisement

**Technology** To use gadgets such as digital cameras and printers to create an advertisement

**Bloom's Taxonomy** Applying and Evaluating

### Prerequisites

- Practice finding and using fractions.
- Study the way artists use elements to create emphasis.
- Review the use of a digital camera and a printer.

### Additional Applications

**Language Arts** Poetry
**Science** Healthy Food Choices
**Scale UP** Have students add text and other graphics to their photographs.
**Scale BACK** Have students use existing products in their advertisements.

### Materials

copies of the "Emphasis: Create an Advertisement" Warm-Up and Directions, pp. 84 and 85 • computers with Internet access and printers • digital cameras • empty cereal or other cardboard boxes • large sheets of drawing paper • pencils • colored pencils • markers • nontoxic glue **Safety!** safety scissors • elements to be used in photograph setups, such as cereal bowls, cereal, and so on

**Alternate Materials:** 35mm cameras

### Web Resources

- http://pbskids.org/dontbuyit/advertisingtricks/
- http://www.foodnavigator.com/news/news-NG.asp?id=53554v
- http://www.media-awareness.ca/english/resources/educational/handouts/advertising_marketing/food_ad_strategies.cfm

**1.** Complete the **Warm-Up** activity on page 84. Review fractions of objects and sets of objects. Review the use of art elements to create emphasis. Demonstrate how to upload photos from a digital camera. Alternatively, have students use 35mm cameras to create images for their advertisements.

**2.** Distribute the **Directions** on page 85. Distribute the materials when students get to Step 3. Assist students if they struggle with creating the fraction. The fraction should be $\frac{5}{15}$ or $\frac{1}{3}$. Help students come up with different ways to showcase their products in their advertisements.

**3.** Have students share their advertisements with the class.

**4.** Complete the assessment rubric on page 85.

**Math Standard:** The student uses fraction names and symbols to describe fractional parts of whole objects or sets of objects.
**Fine Arts Standard:** The student identifies art elements such as color, texture, form, line, space, and value and art principles such as emphasis, pattern, rhythm, balance, proportion, and unity in artwork.
**Technology Standard:** The student accesses remote equipment on a network such as a printer or other peripherals.
**Bloom's Taxonomy:** Applying—use researched advertising methods in an advertisement
Evaluating—judge worth of participation using defined criteria

CHAPTER 8 Fractions • Emphasis

Name _____  Date _____

Activity 1
Warm-Up
Chapter 8

**Emphasis**

# Create an Advertisement

### FOCUS

Completely fill in the bubble of the best answer for each item below.

**Math**
If Judah had 9 raisins, and he ate 3 of them, what fraction describes the amount he has left?

Ⓐ $\frac{1}{2}$
Ⓑ $\frac{1}{8}$
Ⓒ $\frac{1}{3}$
Ⓓ $\frac{2}{3}$

**Fine Arts**
When artists use color to create emphasis in paintings, it means they

Ⓕ direct a viewer's attention.
Ⓖ make paintings seem dull.
Ⓗ use no color.
Ⓙ use only bright colors.

**Technology**
All of the following are input devices **EXCEPT**

Ⓚ a digital camera.
Ⓛ a hand-held computer.
Ⓜ a scanner.
Ⓝ a printer.

### PLAN

1. Think about your favorite cereal. On a separate sheet of paper, make a list of reasons you like it.

2. Describe a commercial or print advertisement you have seen for your favorite cereal or for another similar cereal.

3. Pick one reason you like the cereal. Draw an ad for the cereal that relates to this reason.

Name _____ Date _____

Activity 1
Directions
Chapter 8

**Emphasis**

# Create an Advertisement

**CREATE**

Follow these steps to create an advertisement for a product.

☐ 1. Go to *http://pbskids.org/dontbuyit/advertisingtricks/*.

☐ 2. Imagine that you have been asked to design the package of a new healthy cereal. The cereal has only 5 grams of sugar per serving instead of the 15 grams in many cereals. Write this number as a fraction.

☐ 3. Create your design. Include a graphic explaining that this cereal has less sugar. Write the fraction from Step 2 as the smallest equivalent fraction, and include it in the graphic.

☐ 4. Use color in your design to create emphasis. Cut out your design, and glue it to the front of the cereal box.

☐ 5. Set up and take digital photographs using objects and other students in the classroom. Use positioning to create emphasis.

☐ 6. Upload your photographs onto the computer. Print the best one, and add it to your design.

☐ 7. Complete the assessment rubric.

**CHECK**

| Math Skills | Point Value | My Score | FINAL SCORE |
|---|---|---|---|
| Write a fraction. (Step 2) | 5 | | |

| Fine Arts Skills | Point Value | My Score | FINAL SCORE |
|---|---|---|---|
| Create a photographic advertisement, using emphasis. (Steps 3–6) | 5 | | |

| Technology Skills | Point Value | My Score | FINAL SCORE |
|---|---|---|---|
| Upload photographs. (Step 6) | 5 | | |

TOTAL SCORE _____

Teacher's Initials _____

ACROSS THE CURRICULUM Math Connections

# Activity 2

## Careers in Math

**M**arket researchers must be skilled in both math and analysis, as they use a variety of qualitative and quantitative research techniques to study consumer behavior. Market researchers may use methods such as surveys, tracking systems, focus groups, and demographic models. Companies use the results of market research to make decisions in areas such as product development, packaging, and advertising.

**Examples** — LANGUAGE ARTS WebQuest

# Categorize Toy Advertisements

## Objectives

**Math** To reinforce studies of halves, fourths, and eighths by using them to express time and size

**Language Arts** To reinforce studies of the use of examples by categorizing examples of toy advertisements

**Technology** To use a database program to categorize toy advertisements

**Bloom's Taxonomy** Understanding and Analyzing

## Prerequisites

- Practice identifying fractions, including halves, fourths, and eighths.
- Practice using examples in writing.
- Review how to use a computer database program to categorize information.

## Additional Applications

**Social Studies** Production of a Product

**Fine Arts** Emphasis

**Scale UP** Have students write a paper comparing two toy advertisements.

**Scale BACK** Have students identify characteristics in one toy advertisement.

## Materials

📄 copies of the "Examples: Categorize Toy Advertisements" WebQuest, pp. 88–91 • computers with Internet access and database programs • television with a VCR or DVD player • videotape or DVD with toy ads • print ads from magazines and newspapers • rulers

## WebQuest Map

**Task:**
Videotape of a television toy advertisement and copy of a print toy advertisement

**Process:**

STEP 2 http://www.kbtoys.com/

STEP 3 http://www.focusonyourchild.com/entertain/art1/A0000228.html
http://www.littlekidstuff.com/advertising_and_your_child_article.htm

STEP 4 http://www.ppu.org.uk/chidren/advertising_toys_eu.html

STEP 5 http://www.media-awareness.ca/english/resources/educational/handouts/advertising_marketing/common_ad_strats.cfm

1. **Distribute the WebQuest** on pages 88–91. Have students give examples of toy advertisements. Discuss types of advertisements, such as television, magazine, newspaper, and Internet. Review halves, fourths, and eighths. Review how to create and use a database to categorize information.

2. For the **Task,** record an example of a television toy advertisement. Find an example of a print toy advertisement.

3. Show students examples of half-page, third-page, quarter-page, and other sized ads in magazines and newspapers.

4. Complete the assessment rubric on page 91.

**Math Standard:** The student uses fraction names and symbols to describe fractional parts of whole objects or sets of objects.
**Language Arts Standard:** The student takes simple notes from relevant sources such as classroom guests, information books, and media sources.
**Technology Standard:** The student uses appropriate software to solve problems including the use of databases.
**Bloom's Taxonomy:** Understanding—categorize toy advertising Analyzing—organize information in a database

CHAPTER 8 Fractions • Examples

Name _____ Date _____

Activity 2

**Examples**

# Categorize Toy Advertisements

> **INTRODUCTION**
>
> It has been estimated that the average American child watches as many as 40,000 television advertisements each year. Many of these advertisements are for toys. Toy advertisements are a source to introduce children to new toys and what the toys can do. However, some adults are concerned that advertisements may exaggerate a toy's performance, not show the skills needed to operate a toy, or show pieces that are not included with the toy. Toy advertisements appear in a variety of media, including television, magazines, newspapers, and the Internet. You are going to find and categorize examples of toy advertising and use math to express advertisement measurements.

ACROSS THE CURRICULUM Math Connections

Name _____  Date _____

**Examples**

# Categorize Toy Advertisements

> **TASK**
>
> You work in the advertising department of a toy company. Your company is planning to create a new advertisement, but first they want information on their competitors' advertising. Your job is to work within a team to find examples of your competitors' current advertisements and categorize and organize the advertisements in a database. You will then write recommendations to your company for the creation of their new advertisement.
>
> The specific question you have to consider is *What characteristics can I use to categorize toy advertisements in a database?*
>
> Before you begin your individual research, watch an example of a television toy advertisement, and view an example of a print toy advertisement as a class. Discuss similarities and differences between the two advertisements.

Activity 2
WEB QUEST
Chapter 8

Name _____ Date _____

Activity 2
**WEB QUEST**
Chapter 8

**Examples**

# Categorize Toy Advertisements

**PROCESS**

Follow these steps to categorize toy advertisements.

☐ 1. View examples of television and print toy advertisements. Take notes on each advertisement, such as the length of the television ad and the page size of the print ad.

☐ 2. Go to *http://www.kbtoys.com/* to find examples of Internet toy advertisements. Take notes on each advertisement.

☐ 3. Go to *http://www.focusonyourchild.com/entertain/ art1/A0000228.html* and *http://www.littlekidstuff.com/ advertising_and_your_child_article.htm,* and read about advertising and children. As a group, share the examples of ads you found, and discuss how the ideas in the articles apply to your group's ad examples.

☐ 4. Go to *http://www.ppu.org.uk/chidren/advertising_toys_eu .html* to read about European views on advertising and children.

☐ 5. Go to *http://www.media-awareness.ca/english/resources/ educational/handouts/advertising_marketing/ common_ad_strats.cfm* to read a list of common advertising strategies. Identify the advertising strategy used in each of your examples.

☐ 6. Open the database program on your computer. Create a field for each characteristic your group decided on.

☐ 7. Within your group, take turns entering each example you found as a new record. Express measurements of minutes, pages, and inches in halves, fourths, and eighths.

☐ 8. Write a one-page paper giving recommendations to your company on the creation of their new toy advertisement. Use examples from your group database to support your recommendations.

☐ 9. Complete the assessment rubric.

ACROSS THE CURRICULUM Math Connections

Name _____ Date _____

**Activity 2**
**WEB QUEST**
**Chapter 8**

**Examples**

# Categorize Toy Advertisements

## EVALUATION

| Math Skills | Point Value | My Score | FINAL SCORE |
|---|---|---|---|
| Record time and size measurements. (Step 1) | 2 | | |
| Express measurements in halves, fourths, and eighths. (Step 7) | 3 | | |
| **Language Arts Skills** | **Point Value** | **My Score** | **FINAL SCORE** |
| Find and organize examples. (Steps 1, 2, 6, and 7) | 2 | | |
| Use examples in writing. (Step 8) | 3 | | |
| **Technology Skills** | **Point Value** | **My Score** | **FINAL SCORE** |
| Enter a URL and view a Web page. (Steps 2–5) | 2 | | |
| Use a database to categorize and organize information. (Steps 6 and 7) | 3 | | |

**TOTAL SCORE** _____
Teacher's Initials _____

## CONCLUSION

Answer the following questions on a separate sheet of paper.

1. How did you express the measurements of the advertisements?
2. Did you find more examples of television, print, or Internet advertising?
3. Was a database a good way to categorize and organize your examples? What would be another way to do this?

ACROSS THE CURRICULUM Math Connections

## Activity 1

### History of Math

**P**eople throughout history have used songs to help pass the time and to make work more fun. Sailors used sea shanties with rhythms to match their work, such as a halyard shanty, which has stressed words to accentuate the pull of a rope when raising sails. People laying railroad track used songs to time group lifting of track. Many traditional work songs have become popular camp sing-along songs.

Music

# Evaluate Campfire Songs

## Objectives

**Math** To reinforce studies of measurement by measuring the length of a musical program

**Fine Arts** To reinforce studies of music by creating a campfire song program

**Technology** To use computer basics to view and search Web sites for information

**Bloom's Taxonomy** Analyzing and Creating

## Prerequisites

- Practice measuring elapsed time.
- Review the types of criteria used to evaluate a musical performance.
- Review computer basics, such as opening and closing a program and using the Find feature.

## Additional Applications

**Social Studies** American History
**Language Arts** Rhyme
**Scale UP** Have student groups research and present historical background for their campfire songs.
**Scale BACK** Have students create programs that are only five minutes long.

## Materials

copies of the "Music: Evaluate Campfire Songs" WebQuest, pp. 94–97 • computers with Internet access and printers • headphones • wood or stones to create a "campfire" • stopwatches

**Alternate Materials:** books and recordings of camp and folk songs **eMathTools Stopwatch Tool**

## WebQuest Map

**Task:**
"More Thoughts about Campfires," article giving advice about the types of songs to be sung around a campfire,
http://www.chsscout.net/rescenter/docs/more-cf.shtm

**Process:**

STEP 1 http://memory.loc.gov/ammem/ndlpedu/collections/conserv/history.html

STEP 2 http://memory.loc.gov/ammem/lohtml/lorecexp.html

STEP 3 http://www.ultimatecampingsource.site/camp-activities/classic-camp-songs.page-1.html

STEP 4 http://www.kididdles.com/mouseum/subject.html

1. Distribute the **WebQuest** on pages 94–97. Review how to use a stopwatch to measure elapsed time. Discuss musical performances, and identify types of criteria used in evaluating performances. Review how to use the Find feature in a Web browser. Demonstrate how to print a Web page.

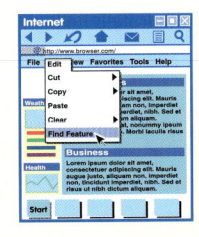

2. Find the online article "More Thoughts about Campfires." Read it aloud, and have students discuss the writer's opinions about effective types of campfire songs.

3. Divide students into small groups. Make sure computers have working speakers or multiple headphone jacks and that the volume is turned up.

4. Provide students with time and areas in which to practice their programs.

5. Clear a large space in the classroom, and set up a "campfire" using wood or stones. Have students gather around it, and allow groups to share their song programs with the class.

6. Complete the assessment rubric on page 97.

**Math Standard:** The student measures to solve problems involving length, area, temperature, and time.
**Fine Arts Standard:** The student defines basic criteria for evaluating musical performances.
**Technology Standard:** The student uses menu options and commands.
**Bloom's Taxonomy:** Analyzing—select songs that represent diverse genres
Creating—organize a group of songs to create a sing-along program

CHAPTER 9 Measurement • Music

93

Name _____ Date _____

**Music**

# Evaluate Campfire Songs

## INTRODUCTION

The history of the camping movement in America followed closely with the history of the conservation movement. As cities grew bigger and bigger at the end of the 1800s, many people began to look for a way to go and enjoy nature. Conservationists worked to make sure natural areas were kept clean and untouched, while leaders in the scouting movement created camps and organizations so children could experience and learn more about the great outdoors. Campfires, used to keep warm and cook food, also became a traditional place for campers to gather and sing songs, tell stories, and perform skits. You will research campfire songs and traditional folk songs and create a program of campfire songs.

Activity 1
Web Quest
Chapter 9

ACROSS THE CURRICULUM Math Connections

Name _____  Date _____

**Activity 1**
**WEB QUEST**
**Chapter 9**

**Music**

# Evaluate Campfire Songs

> **TASK**
>
> You are a camp counselor. You and a group of counselors have been assigned the job of choosing songs for a campfire sing-along. The camp's director wants you to choose several different types of songs, some of which reflect the history of folk songs. You will first research the history of the camping movement and folk songs in America, and then select songs from online databases. You will then create evaluation criteria and organize a program that is less than ten minutes long.
>
> The specific question you have to consider is *What types of songs would work best at a campfire sing-along?*
>
> Before you begin your research, listen as your teacher reads the article "More Thoughts about Campfires." Discuss the types of songs that were recommended.

ACROSS THE CURRICULUM Math Connections          95

**Name** _____ **Date** _____

Activity 1
**WEB QUEST**
Chapter 9

## Music

# Evaluate Campfire Songs

**PROCESS**

Follow these steps to evaluate campfire songs.

☐ 1. Go to *http://memory.loc.gov/ammem/ndlpedu/collections/conserv/history.html,* and listen as your teacher reads about the history of the camping and conservation movements.

☐ 2. Go to *http://memory.loc.gov/ammem/lohtml/lorecexp.html.* Use the Find feature to find links to **children's songs.** Click these links, and listen to the recordings.

☐ 3. Go to *http://www.ultimatecampingsource.site/camp-activities/classic-camp-songs.page-1.html,* and click the song title links to see lyrics and hear music for many sing-along songs. Compare them with the songs from Step 2. Take notes on songs you could use in your campfire program.

☐ 4. Go to *http://www.kididdles.com/mouseum/subject.html,* and scroll down to find links to songs organized by subject. Take notes on songs you might use.

☐ 5. As a group, define three criteria on which to evaluate your campfire song program.

☐ 6. Make a list of possible songs. Print the words from the Web sites, and practice singing them as a group. Use a stopwatch to make sure your program will be less than ten minutes. You can use the *eMathTools: Stopwatch Tool.*

☐ 7. Share and invite other people to join in your songs at the class "campfire." Using your group's criteria, evaluate your performance and selections.

☐ 8. Complete the assessment rubric.

ACROSS THE CURRICULUM Math Connections

Name _____ Date _____

Activity 1
WEB QUEST
Chapter 9

**Music**

# Evaluate Campfire Songs

## EVALUATION

| Math Skills | Point Value | My Score | FINAL SCORE |
|---|---|---|---|
| Select songs to fit a given amount of time. (Step 6) | 1 | | |
| Use a stopwatch to measure the elapsed time of a program. (Step 6) | 4 | | |
| **Fine Arts Skills** | **Point Value** | **My Score** | **FINAL SCORE** |
| Create evaluation criteria with which to judge a musical performance. (Step 5) | 2 | | |
| Apply evaluation criteria to a performance. (Step 7) | 3 | | |
| **Technology Skills** | **Point Value** | **My Score** | **FINAL SCORE** |
| Enter a URL and view a Web page. (Steps 1–4) | 2 | | |
| Use the Find feature in a Web page. (Step 2) | 3 | | |

**TOTAL SCORE** _____

Teacher's Initials _____

## CONCLUSION

Answer the following questions on a separate sheet of paper.
1. How long was your program? How did you measure the time?
2. What type of campfire song do you like best? Why?
3. Why do you think people sing songs around campfires?

ACROSS THE CURRICULUM Math Connections

## Activity 2

### Profiles in Math

**T**he government has always had to balance Americans' economic and recreational needs. In 1965, President Lyndon Johnson gave a speech in which he said America needed a national system of trails so that people could hike and camp in both urban and rural environments. Because of his work, Congress eventually passed the National Trails System Act, setting apart several types of trails for Americans to enjoy.

**Environment** SCIENCE

# Plan a Family Camping Trip

## Objectives

**Math** To reinforce studies of choosing the correct unit by choosing units to measure distance

**Science** To reinforce studies of environment by considering the environment of a camping trip

**Technology** To use a word processing program to create a camping plan and a checklist

**Bloom's Taxonomy** Analyzing and Applying

## Prerequisites

- Practice choosing correct units for measurement situations.
- Study natural environments.
- Review how to create lists in a word processing program.

## Additional Applications

**Social Studies** National Parks

**Language Arts** Creating an Outline

**Scale UP** Have students calculate the approximate amount of gasoline needed for the trip, based on a given number of miles per gallon.

**Scale BACK** Have students plan only the food needed for the camping trip.

## Materials

copies of the "Environment: Plan a Family Camping Trip" Warm-Up and Directions, pp. 100 and 101 • computers with Internet access, word processing programs, and printers • road maps of the United States • rulers

**Alternate Materials:** print resources about camping • writing paper • pencils

## Web Resources

- http://data2.itc.nps.gov/parksearch/geosearch.cfm
- http://www.camping-usa.com/checklist.html
- http://www.suite101.com/article.cfm/camping/34373

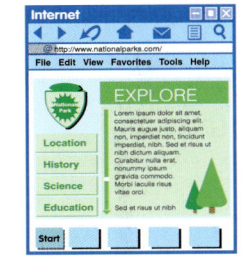

**1.** Complete the **Warm-Up** activity on page 100. Review factors to take into consideration when selecting units of measurement. Review how environments affect people and animals. Demonstrate how to create a bulleted list in a word processing program. Alternatively, have students use print resources to research their trips, and have them create their camping plans using writing paper.

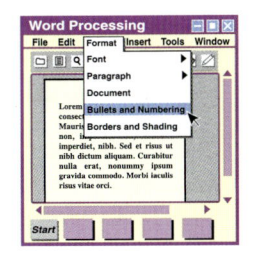

**2.** Distribute the **Directions** on page 101. Tell students to plan trips for their own families or for friends' families. Help them select national parks that include campgrounds. Their estimates of distance can be fairly rough; the focus should be on choosing a unit of measure.

**3.** Have students share their camping plans with the class.

**4.** Complete the assessment rubric on page 101.

**Math Standard:** The student selects and uses appropriate units and procedures to measure length and area.

**Science Standard:** The student knows that living organisms need food, water, light, air, a way to dispose of waste, and an environment in which to live.

**Technology Standard:** The student demonstrates touch keyboarding techniques for operating the alphabetic, numeric, punctuation, and symbol keys as grade-level appropriate.

**Bloom's Taxonomy:** Analyzing—organize camping gear into a planning checklist
Applying—use studies of units of measurement in a real-world context

**CHAPTER 9 Measurement • Environment**

99

Name _____ Date _____

**Activity 2**
**Warm-Up**
**Chapter 9**

**Environment**

# Plan a Family Camping Trip

> **FOCUS**
>
> Completely fill in the bubble of the best answer for each item below.
>
> **Math**
> If you are planning to drive from Virginia to California, the best unit to measure the distance is
>
> - Ⓐ inches.
> - Ⓑ miles.
> - Ⓒ liters.
> - Ⓓ feet.
>
> **Science**
> If a baby bird lives in a nest in a tree, the tree and the nest are its
>
> - Ⓕ environment.
> - Ⓖ family.
> - Ⓗ learned characteristics.
> - Ⓙ basic needs.
>
> **Technology**
> To make a numbered list, you can select
>
> - Ⓚ **Spelling and Grammar** from the **Tools** menu.
> - Ⓛ **Bullets and Numbering** from the **Format** menu.
> - Ⓜ **Borders and Shading** from the **Format** menu.
> - Ⓝ **Header and Footer** from the **View** menu.

**PLAN**

1. On a separate sheet of paper, make a list of ten things you think a family would need on a camping trip.
2. Plan what the family would need to do to get ready for a camping trip. Write each step in order.

100                                    ACROSS THE CURRICULUM Math Connections

Name _____ Date _____

Activity 2

Directions

Chapter 9

**Environment**

# Plan a Family Camping Trip

**CREATE**

Follow these steps to plan a family camping trip.

☐ 1. Go to *http://data2.itc.nps.gov/parksearch/geosearch.cfm.* Choose one of the National Parks in your state.

☐ 2. Click **Plan Your Visit.** Research the camping options for a three-day summer trip as well as the weather and the climate. Find out what fees you will need to pay.

☐ 3. Approximate how far you will travel to the campsite. Choose an appropriate unit of measure.

☐ 4. Go to *http://www.camping-usa.com/checklist.html.* Take notes.

☐ 5. Open a new word processing document. Write a paragraph explaining where you will be camping and how far you will travel. Describe the park environment.

☐ 6. Make a bulleted packing checklist. Include fees.

☐ 7. Edit your camping plan. Save and print the document.

☐ 8. Complete the assessment rubric.

**CHECK**

| Math Skills | Point Value | My Score | FINAL SCORE |
|---|---|---|---|
| Choose and use an appropriate unit of measure. (Steps 3 and 5) | 5 | | |
| **Science Skills** | Point Value | My Score | FINAL SCORE |
| Research a camping environment. (Steps 2 and 4) | 5 | | |
| **Technology Skills** | Point Value | My Score | FINAL SCORE |
| Create a bulleted list in a word processing program. (Step 6) | 5 | | |

TOTAL SCORE _____

Teacher's Initials _____

ACROSS THE CURRICULUM Math Connections

# Activity 1

## Careers in Math

**A**rchitectural engineers apply scientific and engineering principles to the design and construction of buildings and building systems. They emphasize engineering aspects during the design and construction of buildings. Architectural engineers are required to be skilled in the structural, mechanical, and electrical processes of construction, and they must possess a strong knowledge of math, science, and engineering.

**Note Taking • LANGUAGE ARTS**

# Research Monuments around the World

### Objectives

**Math** To reinforce studies of metric measure by researching measurements of monuments

**Language Arts** To reinforce studies of note taking by taking notes about monuments around the world

**Technology** To use electronic references to research monuments around the world

**Bloom's Taxonomy** Understanding and Analyzing

### Prerequisites

- Practice solving problems with meters and centimeters.
- Practice various methods of taking notes.
- Review how to use electronic references.

### Additional Applications

**Social Studies** Washington, D.C.
**Fine Arts** Form
**Scale UP** Have students write a research paper comparing world monuments.
**Scale BACK** Have students take notes on one article about a monument.

### Materials

copies of the "Note Taking: Research Monuments around the World" Warm-Up and Directions, pp. 104 and 105 • electronic reference CD-ROMs • note cards

**Alternate Materials:** print resources such as encyclopedias

### Web Resources

- http://www.yourchildlearns.com/monuments.htm
- http://www.wmf.org/html/programs/watch.html
- http://www.allmath.com/metrictable.php

1. Complete the **Warm-Up** activity on page 104. Practice measuring items using meters and centimeters. Review note taking, and discuss how note taking is useful in conducting research. Review how to insert and run an electronic reference CD-ROM.

2. Distribute the **Directions** on page 105, and give each student a stack of note cards. Have students use various CD-ROMs to research monuments around the world and take notes. Demonstrate how to record the source along with the note on a note card.

3. Remind students to take notes on the measurements of each monument they research.

4. Have students use their notes to organize and list the monuments by continent and by height in meters and centimeters.

5. Discuss how students used note cards to take notes.

6. Complete the assessment rubric on page 105.

**Math Standard:** The student estimates and measures lengths using standard units such as inch, foot, yard, centimeter, decimeter, and meter.
**Language Arts Standard:** The student organizes information in systematic ways, including notes, charts, and labels.
**Technology Standard:** The student uses a variety of input devices such as a mouse, keyboard, disk drive, modem, scanner, digital video, CD-ROM, or touch screen.
**Bloom's Taxonomy:** Understanding—summarize information to take notes
Analyzing—organize notes in a list

CHAPTER 10 Decimals • Note Taking

**Name** _____ **Date** _____

Activity 1

Warm-Up

Chapter 10

**Note Taking**

# Research Monuments around the World

### FOCUS

Completely fill in the bubble of the best answer for each item below.

**Math**
One meter is equal to

- (A) 10 centimeters.
- (B) 100 millimeters.
- (C) 5 decimeters.
- (D) 100 centimeters.

**Language Arts**
Note taking is useful in

- (F) conducting research.
- (G) writing a poem.
- (H) solving a math problem.
- (J) writing a journal entry.

**Technology**
All of the following are electronic references **EXCEPT**

- (K) CD-ROMs.
- (L) textbooks.
- (M) the Internet.
- (N) DVD-ROMs.

### PLAN

Choose a page from a classroom reference book such as an encyclopedia or a textbook. Read the page, and take notes on a note card. Write down the source.

104 ACROSS THE CURRICULUM Math Connections

Name _____ Date _____

**Activity 1**

Directions

Chapter 10

**Note Taking**

# Research Monuments around the World

**CREATE**

Follow these steps to research monuments around the world.

☐ 1. Browse a CD-ROM to find information on a monument. Take notes on a note card. Record the source.

☐ 2. Repeat Step 1 to take notes about various monuments. Use a separate note card for each monument.

☐ 3. Insert other reference CD-ROMs, and take notes on other monuments you find. Record the sources.

☐ 4. Organize your note cards by continent, grouping all monuments from one continent together. Make a list organizing the monuments by continent.

☐ 5. Express all measurements in meters and centimeters in decimal form, converting measurements, if necessary. Organize your note cards by tallest to shortest monument. Make a list organizing the monuments by height.

☐ 6. Complete the assessment rubric.

**CHECK**

| Math Skills | Point Value | My Score | FINAL SCORE |
|---|---|---|---|
| Express measurements in meters and centimeters. (Step 5) | 5 | | |
| **Language Arts Skills** | Point Value | My Score | FINAL SCORE |
| Take notes on note cards. (Steps 1-3) | 5 | | |
| **Technology Skills** | Point Value | My Score | FINAL SCORE |
| Use electronic references to conduct research. (Steps 1-3) | 5 | | |

TOTAL SCORE _____

Teacher's Initials _____

ACROSS THE CURRICULUM Math Connections

**Activity 2**

### Profiles in Math

Christopher Latham Sholes invented the machine called the *Type-Writer* in 1872. Its letters were on the ends of rods called *type bars*, which hung in a circle. Sholes redesigned the layout of the letters on the keyboard to produce what we call the *Universal* keyboard. He rearranged the letters using a study of letter-pair frequency prepared by educator Amos Densmore. The keyboard design was included on Sholes's patent granted in 1878.

**Native Americans**

SOCIAL STUDIES WebQuest

# Write about Totem Poles

## Objectives

**Math** To reinforce studies of tenths by creating a $\frac{1}{10}$ scale drawing

**Social Studies** To reinforce studies of Native American cultures by writing about totem poles

**Technology** To reinforce proper keyboarding techniques

**Bloom's Taxonomy** Understanding and Creating

## Prerequisites

- Practice multiplying and dividing by 10.
- Study totem poles as part of Pacific Northwest Native American culture.
- Review proper keyboarding practices.

## Additional Applications

**Language Arts** Folklore
**Science** Basic Needs
**Scale UP** Have students construct a model of a totem pole rather than a drawing.
**Scale BACK** Have students provide details about only one of the figures on their pole.

## Materials

copies of the "Native Americans: Write about Totem Poles" WebQuest, pp. 108–111 • computers with Internet access, word processing programs, and printers • 11″ × 17″ construction paper • pencils • rulers • colored pencils or crayons

## WebQuest Map

**Task:**
Totem Test, http://www.orau.gov/eeo/natamer/natamer.htm

**Process:**
STEP 1  http://collections.ic.gc.ca/time/galler07/frames/totems.htm
STEP 2  http://www.everythingalaska.com/eta.saxtp.html
http://www.virtualguidebooks.com/ThematicLists/TotemPoles.html
STEP 3  http://www.nativeonline.com/totem_poles.htm
http://users.imag.net/~sry.jkramer/nativetotems/default.html

1. Distribute the **WebQuest** on pages 108–111. Practice multiplying and dividing by 10. Study totem poles, and view examples of totem poles. Review proper keyboarding techniques.

2. For Steps 4 and 5 of the **WebQuest,** students may use a 10-meter totem pole as the model. This will produce a scale that is easier to use: 1 meter = 10 meters.

3. For Step 5, students can use symbols that are important to them or the traditional human and animal symbols found on totem poles. Remind students that the most important totems go on the bottom.

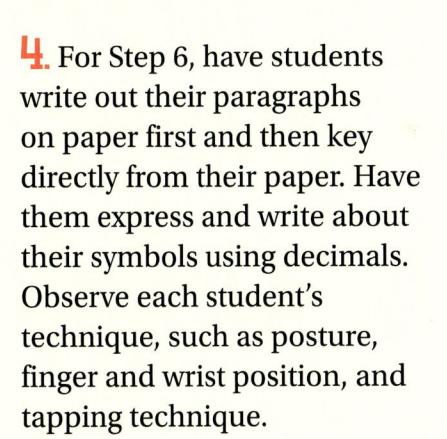

4. For Step 6, have students write out their paragraphs on paper first and then key directly from their paper. Have them express and write about their symbols using decimals. Observe each student's technique, such as posture, finger and wrist position, and tapping technique.

1 meter = 10 meters

5. Complete the assessment rubric on page 111.

**Math Standard:** The student selects and uses appropriate units to measure length.
**Social Studies Standard:** The student explains the significance of selected individual writers and artists and their stories, poems, statues, paintings, and other examples of cultural heritage to communities around the world.
**Technology Standard:** The student demonstrates touch keyboarding techniques for operating the alphabetic keys as grade-level appropriate.
**Bloom's Taxonomy:** Understanding—restate ideas about the meaning of totems
Creating—design a totem pole

CHAPTER 10 Decimals • Native Americans

Name _____ Date _____

**Native Americans**

Activity 2

**WEB QUEST**

Chapter 10

# Write about Totem Poles

### INTRODUCTION

Flags, family crests, and even money contain symbols that have special meanings. Totem poles, found in the Pacific Northwest, also have symbols with special meanings. Native American totem poles were first noticed by European explorers in the 1700s. Totem poles were made for rich and powerful families, and their figures told stories about the families and their wealth. Eventually the art of totem-pole carving died down because of government laws. For a period of time in the early 1900s, few totem poles were created. Today, however, authentic Native American totem-pole carving thrives in British Columbia and southern Alaska.

You are going to learn about the meaning of totem poles and design your own totem pole. You will use math to create the scale. You will then write about your totem pole using a word processing program and proper keyboarding techniques.

ACROSS THE CURRICULUM Math Connections

Name _____ Date _____

**Native Americans**

# Write about Totem Poles

Activity 2

Chapter 10

> **TASK**
>
> You have won a prize in a contest. A wood-carver is going to make a personal totem pole for you. However, you must tell the carver exactly what to make. It can have any design you want. First you will research totem poles to find out why they are made and what the symbols mean. Then you will design your own totem pole and write about it.
>
> The specific questions you have to consider are *What do the symbols on totem poles mean,* and *Which symbols will I put on my pole?*
>
> Before you begin your individual research, go to *http://www.orau.gov/eeo/natamer/natamer.htm,* and take the Totem Test to test your basic knowledge of totem poles.

ACROSS THE CURRICULUM Math Connections           109

Name _____ Date _____  Activity 2

**Native Americans**

# Write about Totem Poles

## PROCESS

Follow these steps to write about your own totem-pole design.

- ☐ 1. Go to *http://collections.ic.gc.ca/time/galler07/frames/totems.htm*.
- ☐ 2. Go to *http://www.everythingalaska.com/eta.saxtp.html* and *http://www.virtualguidebooks.com/ThematicLists/TotemPoles.html* to view totem poles.
- ☐ 3. Go to *http://www.nativeonline.com/totem_poles.htm* and *http://users.imag.net/~sry.jkramer/nativetotems/default.html* to find out what figures on totem poles mean.
- ☐ 4. Decide upon a size for your totem pole. A totem pole is generally anywhere from 10 to 40 meters. Your drawing should have a scale of $\frac{1}{10}$.
- ☐ 5. Draw your totem pole. Use images that have importance in your life or that say something about your personality.
- ☐ 6. Open a new word processing file. Write one paragraph to describe each symbol. Express the measurements of each of the symbols in relationship to the entire totem pole. Write the measurements as decimals. Use proper keyboarding techniques.
- ☐ 7. Format your document. Add a title. Print your document, and attach it to your picture.
- ☐ 8. Complete the assessment rubric.

Name _____ Date _____    Activity 2

**Native Americans**

# Write about Totem Poles

## EVALUATION

| Math Skills | Point Value | My Score | FINAL SCORE |
|---|---|---|---|
| Use the correct measurement in a scale drawing. (Step 4) | 2 | | |
| Create and describe measurements for a totem pole using the scale of $\frac{1}{10}$. (Steps 4 and 6) | 3 | | |
| **Social Studies Skills** | **Point Value** | **My Score** | **FINAL SCORE** |
| Research the use of totem poles in Native American culture. (Step 1) | 2 | | |
| Describe what the symbols on totem poles mean. (Steps 3 and 6) | 3 | | |
| **Technology Skills** | **Point Value** | **My Score** | **FINAL SCORE** |
| Key a document in a word processing file. (Step 6) | 2 | | |
| Use proper keyboarding techniques. (Step 6) | 3 | | |

**TOTAL SCORE** _____

Teacher's Initials _____

## CONCLUSION

Answer the following questions on a separate sheet of paper.

1. What were the measurements for your totem pole? How did you get those measurements?
2. What do the figures on your totem pole mean?

ACROSS THE CURRICULUM Math Connections

Activity 1

## Profiles in Math

**W**hen Lewis and Clark made their famous exploration through western North America, they were asked to make maps of their journey. William Clark, the head cartographer, had many instruments, but most of them could only measure short distances. For much of the trip, Clark simply used a compass to take visual bearings at each new turn. Despite crude methods, Clark created amazingly accurate maps.

**Balance** ART

# Create a Map of Your Neighborhood

## Objectives

**Math** To reinforce studies of polygons by using polygons in a map design

**Fine Arts** To reinforce studies of the principle of balance by using balance in a map design

**Technology** To use a drawing and graphics program to create a map of a neighborhood

**Bloom's Taxonomy** Remembering and Creating

## Prerequisites

- Practice identifying the characteristics of polygons.
- Study the use of balance in art and design.
- Review the use of a drawing and graphics program.

## Additional Applications

**Social Studies** Maps
**Science** Magnets
**Scale UP** Have students add topographical features to their maps.
**Scale BACK** Have students create maps of the school building.

## Materials

copies of the "Balance: Create a Map of Your Neighborhood" Warm-Up and Directions, pp. 114 and 115 • computers with Internet access, drawing and graphics programs, and printers • compasses • graph paper • pencils

**Alternate Materials:** drawing paper • markers • books about maps and map elements

## Web Resources

- http://pr.utk.edu/ut2kids/maps/map.html
- http://collections.ic.gc.ca/allaboutmaps/aaMaps_M3_elements_Z.htm
- http://www.nps.gov/jeff/LewisClark2/TheJourney/Mapmaking.htm

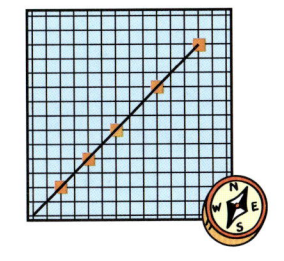

**1.** Complete the **Warm-Up** activity on page 114. Review characteristics of polygons. Discuss the use of balance in artwork, and have students identify examples from artwork in books or on the Internet. Review how to use the tools in a drawing and graphics program. If computers are not available, have students use books about maps and map elements and create their maps using drawing paper and markers.

**2.** Distribute the **Directions** on page 115. The content of the Web sites is above level; read sections aloud as needed.

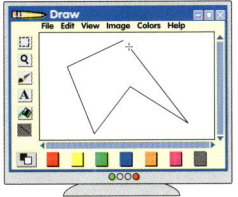

**3.** Demonstrate how to use a compass, and have students practice reading a compass in class. Create a sign-out sheet for the compasses, and allow students to take turns borrowing them to use in their neighborhood maps.

**4.** Have students share their maps with the class.

**5.** Complete the assessment rubric on page 115.

**Math Standard:** The student names, describes, and compares shapes and solids using formal geometric vocabulary.
**Fine Arts Standard:** The student develops a variety of effective compositions, using design skills.
**Technology Standard:** The student publishes information in a variety of media including, but not limited to, printed copy.
**Bloom's Taxonomy:** Remembering—recall research information about map elements
Creating—use polygons to create symbols that represent places in a neighborhood

CHAPTER 11 Geometry • Balance

113

Name _____ Date _____

*Activity 1*
*Warm-Up*
*Chapter 11*

**Balance**

# Create a Map of Your Neighborhood

**FOCUS**

Completely fill in the bubble of the best answer for each item below.

**Math**
A polygon is a shape that has

- Ⓐ three or more sides.
- Ⓑ no sides.
- Ⓒ less than two sides.
- Ⓓ sides that do not connect.

**Fine Arts**
When an artwork has asymmetrical balance, the two sides

- Ⓕ are exactly the same.
- Ⓖ are not the same but have the same visual weight.
- Ⓗ are arranged around a circle.
- Ⓙ have no visual weight.

**Technology**
You can change the color of a shape in a drawing and graphics document by using

- Ⓚ the Fill tool.
- Ⓛ the Line tool.
- Ⓜ the Shape tool.
- Ⓝ the Text Box tool.

**PLAN**

1. Imagine you were going to take someone on a tour of your neighborhood. On a separate sheet of paper, make a list of interesting places and things in your neighborhood.

2. Write down how you could represent these things on a map using simple polygons as symbols.

Name _____ Date _____  Activity 1

**Balance**

Directions

Chapter 11

# Create a Map of Your Neighborhood

**CREATE**

Follow these steps to create a map of your neighborhood.

☐ 1. Go to *http://pr.utk.edu/ut2kids/maps/map.html*.

☐ 2. Go to *http://collections.ic.gc.ca/allaboutmaps/ aaMaps_M3_elements_Z.htm*. Click **Legends and Symbols** and **Compass.**

☐ 3. Sketch a map of two streets in your neighborhood. Make each square on the graph paper equal five of your feet. Make the top of your paper north. Mark important places on the map as you go.

☐ 4. Open a new drawing and graphics document. Create a polygon to mark off the edges of your map. Use the drawing tools to create symbols to mark the important places. Use your sketch as a reference. Use color to fill in the background and create balance.

☐ 5. Draw a symbol key including all the symbols and labels, explaining what they represent. Draw a compass rose. Print your map. Complete the assessment rubric.

**CHECK**

| Math Skills | Point Value | My Score | FINAL SCORE |
|---|---|---|---|
| Use polygons to create symbols. (Steps 4 and 5) | 5 | | |
| Fine Arts Skills | Point Value | My Score | FINAL SCORE |
| Use color to create balance. (Step 4) | 5 | | |
| Technology Skills | Point Value | My Score | FINAL SCORE |
| Use the tools in a drawing and graphics program. (Steps 4 and 5) | 5 | | |

TOTAL SCORE _____

Teacher's Initials _____

ACROSS THE CURRICULUM Math Connections

# Activity 2

## Profiles in Math

**V**itruvius was a Roman writer, architect, and engineer who lived during the first century B.C. Vitruvius wrote *De Architectura*, or *The Ten Books of Architecture*, perhaps the first written work on architecture. The ten books include writings on the principles of architecture, architectural materials, and buildings such as temples, theaters, baths, and public buildings. Vitruvius wrote that symmetry and proportion were fundamental in the design of temples.

Descriptive Writing
**LANGUAGE ARTS WebQuest**

# Create a Presentation about Houses

## Objectives

**Math** To reinforce studies of slides, flips, and turns by describing slides, flips, and turns in architecture

**Language Arts** To reinforce studies of descriptive writing by describing houses around the world

**Technology** To use a presentation program to create a presentation about houses around the world

**Bloom's Taxonomy** Understanding and Creating

## Prerequisites

- Identify slides, flips, and turns in geometric shapes.
- Practice writing descriptively.
- Review how to use a presentation program.

## Additional Applications

**Social Studies** Early Civilizations
**Fine Arts** Texture
**Scale UP** Have students create a multimedia presentation by adding visual elements and sound clips.
**Scale BACK** Have students create one slide for a class presentation.

## Materials

copies of the "Descriptive Writing: Create a Presentation about Houses" WebQuest, pp. 118–121 • computers with Internet access and presentation programs • projector • photo of a house from another part of the world

## WebQuest Map

**Task:**
Photo of a house from another part of the world

**Process:**

STEP 1  http://library.thinkquest.org/10098/

STEP 2  http://www.archkidecture.org/

STEP 3  http://www.hgpho.to/wfest/house/house-e.html

STEP 4  http://user.chollian.net/~ucnet2006/
http://www.washington.edu/ark2/archtm/natlist.html

STEP 5  http://www.clubs.psu.edu/up/aegsa/freegifs.html

1. Distribute the **WebQuest** on pages 118–121. Discuss houses around the world, and have students give examples of different kinds of houses. Review slides, flips, and turns, and discuss how geometry relates to architecture. Review how to use a presentation program.

2. For the **Task,** find a picture of a house from another part of the world from a book, the Internet, or another source, and print or make copies for the class. Distribute copies of the photo, and discuss how the house in the picture is different from the houses in which students live.

3. Students will need to save pictures to their computers or on discs according to your school's policy.

4. Demonstrate for students how to identify geometric slides, flips, and turns in pictures of buildings or architectural ornamentation.

5. Have students use a projector to give their presentations. If a projector is not available, have students print their slides to share with the class.

6. Complete the assessment rubric on page 121.

**Math Standard:** The student names, describes, and compares shapes and solids using formal geometric vocabulary.
**Language Arts Standard:** The student writes for a variety of audiences and purposes and in a variety of forms.
**Technology Standard:** The student uses presentation software to communicate with specific audiences.
**Bloom's Taxonomy:** Understanding—describe houses around the world
Creating—produce a presentation

CHAPTER 11 Geometry • Descriptive Writing

Name _____  Date _____  Activity 2

**Descriptive Writing**

WEB QUEST
Chapter 11

# Create a Presentation about Houses

### INTRODUCTION

People around the world live in all kinds of houses. You might know people that live in one-story houses, two-story houses, apartments, or mobile homes. These are all common American homes. In other countries around the world, it is common for people to live in houses on the water, houses in trees or on stilts, underground houses, or houses made of mud, straw, reeds, or cloth. Houses from other parts of the world might have a structure similar to American houses, but they look different on the outside. You are going to research houses around the world. You will use math to describe different houses.

118                                   ACROSS THE CURRICULUM Math Connections

Name _____ Date _____

Activity 2

**Descriptive Writing**

# Create a Presentation about Houses

> **TASK**
>
> You are an architect who designs houses. You have clients who would like to build a house modeled on a house from another country. However, they do not know what country they want to choose. Your job is to create a presentation to introduce them to architecture and houses around the world.
>
> The specific question you have to consider is *What are houses like around the world?*
>
> Before you begin your individual research, look at a photo of a house from another part of the world. Discuss how the house in the picture is different from your own home and reasons why it might be different.

ACROSS THE CURRICULUM Math Connections

Name _____  Date _____  Activity 2

**Descriptive Writing**

# Create a Presentation about Houses

**PROCESS**

Follow these steps to create a presentation about houses.

☐ 1. Go to *http://library.thinkquest.org/10098/* to research architecture styles.

☐ 2. Go to *http://www.archkidecture.org/*, and click **about structures** to read about different architectural structures. Click **about materials** to read about different building materials.

☐ 3. Go to *http://www.hgpho.to/wfest/house/house-e.html* to view pictures of houses around the world. Choose five houses from different countries to use in your presentation, and save the pictures. Take notes.

☐ 4. Go to *http://user.chollian.net/~ucnet2006/* and *http://www.washington.edu/ark2/archtm/natlist.html,* and find examples of architecture from each country you chose. Save pictures, and take notes.

☐ 5. Go to *http://www.clubs.psu.edu/up/aegsa/freegifs.html* to view examples of architectural ornamentation. Save pictures of any ornamentation that would be used in the countries you are covering.

☐ 6. Open a new presentation program. Create a title slide with the name of the first country you chose. Create another slide, and insert the picture of the house you saved in Step 3. Write a descriptive paragraph about the house. Describe the geometric shapes that make up the house in terms of geometric slides, flips, and turns. Create slides for the other information you found. For pictures of architectural ornamentation, describe the pattern in the picture in terms of slides, flips, and turns. Repeat for each country in your presentation. Share your presentation with the class.

☐ 7. Complete the assessment rubric.

Name _____ Date _____ Activity 2

**Descriptive Writing**

WEB QUEST
Chapter 11

# Create a Presentation about Houses

## EVALUATION

| Math Skills | Point Value | My Score | FINAL SCORE |
|---|---|---|---|
| Identify slides, flips, and turns in pictures. (Step 6) | 2 | | |
| Describe slides, flips, and turns. (Step 6) | 3 | | |
| **Language Arts Skills** | **Point Value** | **My Score** | **FINAL SCORE** |
| Research information for a presentation. (Steps 1–5) | 2 | | |
| Write descriptive text. (Step 6) | 3 | | |
| **Technology Skills** | **Point Value** | **My Score** | **FINAL SCORE** |
| Enter a URL and view a Web page. (Steps 1–5) | 2 | | |
| Use a presentation program to create slides. (Step 6) | 3 | | |

**TOTAL SCORE** _____

Teacher's Initials _____

## CONCLUSION

Answer the following questions on a separate sheet of paper.

1. How are houses around the world different from where you live?

2. How would your presentation help your clients choose a house style? How could presentations be used in other jobs?

3. How is geometry related to architecture? Why would it be important to understand concepts such as slides, flips, and turns if you were an architect?

ACROSS THE CURRICULUM Math Connections

## Activity 1

### History of Math

The Incas developed a method of recording numerical information which involved knots in strings, called a *quipu*. A quipu was a storage device that used knots to represent numbers of objects, such as sheep or cattle. The number of knots in the string determined a specific number in a corresponding unit of 10. Colors were also used to identify what the number was recording.

Animals
SCIENCE WebQuest

# Categorize Sheep Facts

## Objectives

**Math** To reinforce studies of tally marks by using tally charts to categorize sheep facts

**Science** To reinforce studies of animals by researching facts about sheep

**Technology** To use the Internet to research breeds of sheep

**Bloom's Taxonomy** Analyzing and Evaluating

## Prerequisites

- Practice using tally charts and marks.
- Review characteristics of mammals.
- Review how to search the Internet using a browser.

## Additional Applications

**Social Studies** Rural Life

**Fine Arts** Shading

**Scale UP** Have groups create three-dimensional, interactive exhibits.

**Scale BACK** Have students research one breed of sheep only.

## Materials

copies of the "Animals: Categorize Sheep Facts" WebQuest, pp. 124–127 • computers with Internet access and printers • poster board • markers • nontoxic glue Safety! scissors

## WebQuest Map

**Task:**
"Charmingfare Farm Animal Facts: Sheep," an article describing breeds of sheep on a particular farm, http://www.charmingfare.com/animalfacts/sheep.php

**Process:**

STEP 1 http://www.bettybookmark.com/s/sheep.htm

STEP 2 http://www.uga.edu/~lam/kids/sheep/default.html

STEP 3 http://www.kiddyhouse.com/Farm/Sheep

**1.** Distribute the **WebQuest** on pages 124–127. Review how to use tally marks in a tally chart. Review characteristics of mammals. Demonstrate how to perform a regular search and an image search using an Internet search engine.

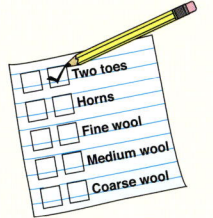

**2.** Find the online article "Charmingfare Farm Animal Facts: Sheep." Read it aloud, and have students discuss other examples of different varieties of the same animal.

**3.** Divide students into small groups. Distribute the materials.

**4.** Help any students who have difficulty selecting breeds and categorizing the animals. You may wish to select a breed and demonstrate how to create a tally chart on the board.

**5.** Complete the assessment rubric on page 127.

**Math Standard:** The student solves problems by collecting, organizing, displaying, and interpreting sets of data.

**Science Standard:** The student observes and identifies characteristics among species that allow each to survive and reproduce.

**Technology Standard:** The student applies appropriate electronic search strategies in the acquisition of information including key word search strategies.

**Bloom's Taxonomy:** Analyzing—organize pieces of information to create a display
Evaluating—judge own participation using specified criteria

CHAPTER 12 Data Analysis and Probability • Animals

123

Name _____ Date _____

Activity 1

**Animals**

# Categorize Sheep Facts

WEB QUEST
Chapter 12

> **INTRODUCTION**
>
> Sheep have been bred for thousands of years. About five thousand years ago, people began spinning sheep's wool to make yarn. Sheep also continue to be raised for their meat and their milk. Today there are over eight hundred different breeds of domesticated, or farmed, sheep. Each breed has special characteristics that allow it to live in a particular climate and environment. You will research breeds of sheep and create an exhibit categorizing facts about them.

ACROSS THE CURRICULUM Math Connections

Name _____ Date _____

**Activity 1**

**Animals**

# Categorize Sheep Facts

**Chapter 12**

> **TASK**
>
> You are a member of a group of farmers who own a large sheep farm. You want to begin allowing groups of students and families to visit the farm and learn more about sheep. To help students learn about sheep breeds on your farm, you are going to design an exhibit. You will research sheep breeds and categorize facts about them. You will then create an exhibit comparing and displaying these facts.
>
> The specific question you have to consider is *How are breeds of sheep similar to and different from each other?*
>
> Before you begin your research, listen as your teacher reads the article "Charmingfare Farm Animal Facts: Sheep." Discuss breeds of sheep and other animals.

ACROSS THE CURRICULUM Math Connections

Name _____  Date _____  Activity 1

**Animals**

WEB QUEST
Chapter 12

# Categorize Sheep Facts

**PROCESS**

Follow these steps to categorize sheep facts.

☐ 1. Go to *http://www.bettybookmark.com/s/sheep.htm,* and read facts about sheep.

☐ 2. Go to *http://www.uga.edu/~lam/kids/sheep/default.html.* Read the information, and look at the pictures. Take some general notes.

☐ 3. Go to *http://www.kiddyhouse.com/Farm/Sheep/,* and read about sheep. Make a list of facts about the physical appearance of different types of sheep. Use tally marks to record how many breeds of sheep apply to each fact.

☐ 4. Choose three breeds of sheep from the Web site. Click the links under *More Sheep Facts* to read about them. Then use an Internet search engine to find more information about them. Make sure to evaluate all Web sites for appropriateness and information.

☐ 5. Do an image search using an Internet search engine to find photographs of the three breeds of sheep you chose. Print those pages.

☐ 6. Using a sheet of poster board, make an exhibit about sheep facts. Organize your information comparing the three breeds of sheep. Create a tally chart, and list facts. Cut out the photographs of the sheep, and glue them onto your board. Add other drawings to make your exhibit more interesting.

☐ 7. Present your exhibit to the class.

☐ 8. Complete the assessment rubric.

126                      ACROSS THE CURRICULUM Math Connections

Name _____ Date _____

Activity 1
WEB QUEST
Chapter 12

**Animals**

# Categorize Sheep Facts

## EVALUATION

| Math Skills | Point Value | My Score | FINAL SCORE |
|---|---|---|---|
| Categorize general sheep facts using tally marks. (Step 3) | 2 | | |
| Categorize facts about sheep breeds using tally marks. (Step 6) | 3 | | |
| **Science Skills** | Point Value | My Score | FINAL SCORE |
| Research facts about sheep. (Steps 1–5) | 2 | | |
| Organize facts in an exhibit display. (Step 6) | 3 | | |
| **Technology Skills** | Point Value | My Score | FINAL SCORE |
| Enter a URL and view a Web page. (Steps 1–3) | 1 | | |
| Use a search engine to find information and images. (Steps 4 and 5) | 4 | | |

TOTAL SCORE _____
Teacher's Initials _____

## CONCLUSION

Answer the following questions on a separate sheet of paper.
1. What was the most interesting thing you learned about sheep?
2. If you could raise one breed of sheep you researched, which would it be? Why?
3. What would you add to your exhibit to make it even more interesting?

ACROSS THE CURRICULUM Math Connections

# Activity 2

## Profiles in Math

**H**ead, *H*eart, *H*ands, and *H*ealth are the four *H*s in 4-H. These are the four values of the program. The original goal of the program was to extend agricultural education to rural youth so that they could "learn by doing." Today, the goal of 4H is the development of youth as individuals and as responsible and productive citizens.

Careers **SOCIAL STUDIES**

# Research Horse Farming

## Objectives

**Math** To reinforce studies of data collection by collecting data about horse farming

**Social Studies** To reinforce studies of careers by researching horse farming

**Technology** To use a spreadsheet program to create a spreadsheet of horse-farming costs

**Bloom's Taxonomy** Analyzing and Applying

## Prerequisites

- Practice collecting and organizing data.
- Study different kinds of careers.
- Review how to use a spreadsheet program.

## Additional Applications

**Language Arts** Write a Persuasive Flyer

**Science** Behaviors

**Scale UP** Have students create a more complex spreadsheet with costs for individual items and subtotals.

**Scale BACK** Provide students with costs to enter into their spreadsheets.

## Materials

copies of the "Careers: Research Horse Farming" Warm-Up and Directions, pp. 130 and 131
- computers with Internet access and spreadsheet programs • paper • pencils

**Alternate Materials:** books about horse care and horse farming

### Web Resources

- http://www.ext.vt.edu/resources/4h/virtualfarm/equine/equine.html
- http://horseweb.com/

**1.** Have students complete the **Warm-Up** activity on page 130. Practice collecting and organizing data. Study different careers, and have students give examples of careers. Review how to use a spreadsheet program.

**2.** Distribute the **Directions** on page 131. If computer access is not available, have students find information using books about horse farming, and have them create their spreadsheets on paper.

**3.** For Steps 3 and 4, allow students to research different breeds and their costs. Find costs on the Internet as a class. Have students make estimates for some of the costs, such as veterinary care.

**4.** Have students format the data cells as currency with two decimal places. Have students enter a SUM formula to total the costs.

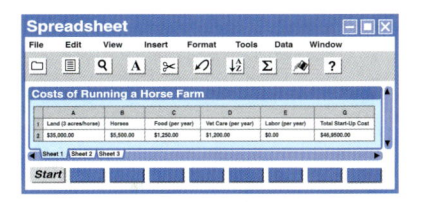

**5.** Complete the assessment rubric on page 131.

**Math Standard:** The student solves problems by collecting, organizing, displaying, and interpreting sets of data.
**Social Studies Standard:** The student identifies ways of earning, spending, and saving money.
**Technology Standard:** The student uses appropriate software to solve problems including the use of spreadsheets.
**Bloom's Taxonomy:** Analyzing—implement a cost study of horse farms
Applying—generate a spreadsheet of costs

CHAPTER 12 Data Analysis and Probability • Careers

129

Name _____ Date _____

Activity 2
Warm-Up
Chapter 12

**Careers**

# Research Horse Farming

## FOCUS

Completely fill in the bubble of the best answer for each item below.

**Math**
What are lines drawn to collect data called?

- Ⓐ verticals
- Ⓑ drawing marks
- Ⓒ tally marks
- Ⓓ list marks

**Social Studies**
Which is **NOT** an example of a career?

- Ⓕ police officer
- Ⓖ playing
- Ⓗ veterinarian
- Ⓙ teacher

**Technology**
Which would you **NOT** use a spreadsheet program for?

- Ⓚ organizing data
- Ⓛ making a chart or graph
- Ⓜ calculating data
- Ⓝ finding a Web site

## PLAN

Imagine that your family is going to start a horse farm. Write down everything that you think your family will have to buy.

_____

_____

_____

_____

_____

ACROSS THE CURRICULUM Math Connections

Name _____ Date _____ Activity 2

**Careers**

Directions

Chapter 12

# Research Horse Farming

**CREATE**

Follow these steps to research horse farming as a career.

☐ 1. Research and find information about horse farmers and horse farming.

☐ 2. Take out your list from the **Warm-Up.**

☐ 3. Decide what kind of farm you will have and how big it will be. Decide what kinds of horses and how many horses will be on the farm.

☐ 4. Find out the costs to run your horse farm.

☐ 5. Create a spreadsheet for the costs of a horse farm. Use your list to make headings. Fill in your spreadsheet with data. Enter a formula to total the costs.

☐ 6. Complete the assessment rubric.

**CHECK**

| Math Skills | Point Value | My Score | FINAL SCORE |
|---|---|---|---|
| Collect data and compare costs involved in horse farming. (Steps 1–5) | 5 | | |
| **Social Studies Skills** | Point Value | My Score | FINAL SCORE |
| Determine the factors involved in horse farming as a career. (Steps 1–4) | 5 | | |
| **Technology Skills** | Point Value | My Score | FINAL SCORE |
| Create and format a spreadsheet. (Step 5) | 5 | | |

**TOTAL SCORE** _____

Teacher's Initials _____

ACROSS THE CURRICULUM Math Connections

131

# Mathematic Research Overview

## Content Strands of Mathematics

The eight content strands of mathematics are integrated into the activities within *Across the Curriculum Math Connections.*

| | | |
|---|---|---|
| **Algebra**<br>Algebra uses symbols to represent arithmetic operations. Algebraic thinking involves understanding patterns, equations, and relationships and includes concepts of functions and inverse operations. Because algebra uses symbols rather than numbers, it can produce general rules that apply to all numbers. | *Across the Curriculum Math Connections* **and Algebra**<br>Students use symbols and mathematical models in the study of patterns, relationships, and functions in a variety of activities. They also analyze change. | **Technology Applications**<br>Keyboarding and Internet activities support algebra concepts. |
| **Arithmetic**<br>Arithmetic includes basic operations with whole numbers: addition, subtraction, multiplication, division, and place holding. | *Across the Curriculum Math Connections* **and Arithmetic**<br>Students use arithmetic operations to record, organize, and communicate ideas in spreadsheets and presentations; to solve problems; and to model real facts or events. | **Technology Applications**<br>Word Processing and Keyboarding activities support arithmetic concepts. |
| **Data Collection and Organization**<br>Data collection and organization is the ability to organize information to make it easier to use and includes the ability to interpret data and graphs. | *Across the Curriculum Math Connections* **and Data Collection and Organization**<br>Students use spreadsheet programs, graphs, and database programs to collect and organize data. They also develop the ability to display relevant data appropriately. | **Technology Applications**<br>Spreadsheet, Database, and Electronic Reference activities support data collection and organization concepts. |
| **Geometry**<br>Geometry deals with the properties of space. Plane geometry is the geometry of flat surfaces; solid geometry is the geometry of three-dimensional space figures. | *Across the Curriculum Math Connections* **and Geometry**<br>Students analyze properties and characteristics of shapes, understand coordinate systems, and apply visual and spatial skills to solve problems. Concrete models, software, and drawings are used to teach geometric concepts. | **Technology Applications**<br>Presentation and Drawing and Graphics activities support geometry concepts. |

| | | |
|---|---|---|
| **Measurement**<br>The measurement strand includes understanding what a measurement is and how units relate to measurement. | *Across the Curriculum Math Connections and Measurement*<br>Students learn and apply units and processes of measurement. They make connections by evaluating the relationships between measurable attributes of objects. | **Technology Applications**<br>Spreadsheet and Drawing and Graphics activities support measurement concepts. |
| **Number Sense and Place Value**<br>Number sense and place value includes the understanding of the significance and use of numbers in counting, measuring, comparing, and ordering. | *Across the Curriculum Math Connections and Number Sense and Place Value*<br>Students develop number sense and computational fluency through an understanding of number and number systems, including the representation of and relationship between numbers. | **Technology Applications**<br>Spreadsheet and Computer Basics activities support number sense and place-value concepts. |
| **Probability and Statistics**<br>Probability and statistics deal with events where outcomes are uncertain and assess the likelihood of possible outcomes. | *Across the Curriculum Math Connections and Probability and Statistics*<br>Students reason statistically by formulating questions, analyzing data, developing inferences, and applying concepts of probability. | **Technology Applications**<br>Gadgets and Spreadsheet activities support probability and statistics concepts. |
| **Rational Numbers**<br>Rational numbers includes the understanding of fractions, decimals, and percentages and their relationships to each other, including the ability to perform calculations and to use rational numbers in measurement. | *Across the Curriculum Math Connections and Rational Numbers*<br>Students develop number sense and computational fluency through an understanding of fractions, decimals, and percentages, including the representation of and relationship between rational numbers. | **Technology Applications**<br>Keyboarding and Word Processing activities support rational numbers concepts. |

# Integrating Math with Other Curriculum

Math learning is enhanced when students see a relationship between mathematics and other subjects and can make a connection between math and their daily lives. If mathematics experiences are presented in different environments and contexts, students will develop the ability to see relationships between mathematical concepts and apply them in a problem-solving context. It is important to build upon prior knowledge and develop concepts gradually over time.

## Integrating Math with Fine Arts

***Across the Curriculum Math Connections*** contains projects which use art to enhance mathematical understanding and meet the guidelines for both disciplines. Students apply mathematical thinking to solve problems within the context of art, music, dance, or theatre. Below are some ways math and fine arts can be integrated.

| Connection | Math | Fine Arts |
|---|---|---|
| symbols | Mathematical symbols communicate ideas such as *more than* (>). | Symbols can be used to communicate ideas in visual art. |
| shape | Geometric shapes can be described and analyzed. | Shape is used in visual art and can be formed by the student's body in dance. |
| pattern | Algebraic thinking involves understanding patterns. | Pattern is used in visual art as repeated surface decoration. |
| measurement | Measurement has real-world application with measurement tools. | Tempo and note value have measurement in music. |

### How We Do It

In *Across the Curriculum Math Connections*, math is integrated with fine arts in the following ways:

1. **Standards are identified.** Standards are met for math and fine arts concepts in all fine arts activities.
2. **The task and assessment are planned.** Complete step-by-step instructions and evaluation rubrics are provided for each activity.
3. **A variety of student needs are met.** Opportunities for customization are provided in each activity.
4. **Opportunities for students to communicate mathematical reasoning are available.** The fine arts present many opportunities for nonstandard mathematical communication in the form of visual art, music, and performance.
5. **Feedback is encouraged.** Activities are structured to provide students an opportunity to incorporate feedback into their projects.

# Integrating Math with Language Arts

***Across the Curriculum Math Connections*** contains projects which use language arts to enhance mathematical understanding and meet the guidelines for both disciplines. Students apply mathematical thinking to solve problems within the context of language arts and reading. Below are some ways math and language arts can be integrated.

| Connection | Math | Language Arts |
| --- | --- | --- |
| sequence | Ordinal numbers name position in math. | Elements of plot can be described using ordinal numbers. |
| variables | Variables allow for the production of general rules for all numbers. | Students explore variables through the revision stages of the writing process. |
| pattern | Algebraic thinking involves understanding patterns. | Pattern is used in poetry. |
| communication | Mathematical symbols communicate ideas, such as *equals*. | The main focus of language arts is the communication of ideas. |

## How We Do It

In *Across the Curriculum Math Connections,* math is integrated with language arts in the following ways:

1. **Standards are identified.** Standards are met for math and language arts concepts in all language arts activities.
2. **The task and assessment are planned.** Complete step-by-step instructions and evaluation rubrics are provided for each activity.
3. **A variety of student needs are met.** Opportunities for customization are provided in each activity.
4. **Opportunities for students to communicate mathematical reasoning are available.** Language arts present many opportunities for nonstandard mathematical communication in the form of poetry, writing, and formal speaking.
5. **Feedback is encouraged.** Activities are structured to provide students an opportunity to incorporate feedback into their projects.

# Integrating Math with Science

***Across the Curriculum Math Connections*** contains projects which use science to enhance mathematical understanding and meet the guidelines for both disciplines. Students apply mathematical thinking to solve problems within the context of science. Below are some ways math and science can be integrated.

| Connection | Math | Science |
|---|---|---|
| data | Graphing skills are used to express data. | Data is compiled and evaluated, often using graphs, diagrams, or charts. |
| variables | Variables allow for the production of general rules for all numbers. | Students explore variables through the revision stages of the writing process. |
| exponential notation | Large numbers are expressed and manipulated using exponential notation. | Scientific notation is a form of exponential notation. |
| graphs | Graphing skills are used to express data. | Data is compiled and evaluated, often using graphs, diagrams, or charts. |

### How We Do It
In *Across the Curriculum Math Connections,* math is integrated with science in the following ways:
1. **Standards are identified.** Standards are met for math and science concepts in all science activities.
2. **The task and assessment are planned.** Complete step-by-step instructions and evaluation rubrics are provided for each activity.
3. **A variety of student needs are met.** Opportunities for customization are provided in each activity.
4. **Opportunities for students to communicate mathematical reasoning are available.** Science presents many opportunities for nonstandard mathematical communication in the form of experiments, diagrams, and charts.
5. **Feedback is encouraged.** Activities are structured to provide students an opportunity to incorporate feedback into their projects.

# Integrating Math with Social Studies

*Across the Curriculum Math Connections* contains projects which use social studies to enhance mathematical understanding and meet the guidelines for both disciplines. Students apply mathematical thinking to solve problems within the context of social studies. Below are some ways math and social studies can be integrated.

| Connection | Math | Social Studies |
| --- | --- | --- |
| time | The concept of time is explored through measurement and data collection and organization. | Time-zone maps require knowledge of the concept of elapsed time. |
| area | Geometric concepts, such as area, help explain algebraic concepts. | The concept of area is used in conjunction with map skills. |
| temperature | Temperature is a real-world application of measurement. | Understanding temperature is vital to understanding the concepts of weather and climate. |
| ratios | The arithmetic concept of ratio is vital to the understanding of the meaning of rates. | Population density can be compared using ratios. |

### How We Do It

In *Across the Curriculum Math Connections,* math is integrated with social studies in the following ways:

1. **Standards are identified.** Standards are met for math and social studies concepts in all social studies activities.
2. **The task and assessment are planned.** Complete step-by-step instructions and evaluation rubrics are provided for each activity.
3. **A variety of student needs are met.** Opportunities for customization are provided in each activity.
4. **Opportunities for students to communicate mathematical reasoning are available.** Social studies present many opportunities for nonstandard mathematical communication in the form of maps, presentations, and writing.
5. **Feedback is encouraged.** Activities are structured to provide students an opportunity to incorporate feedback into their projects.

# Integrating Math with Technology

***Across the Curriculum Math Connections*** contains projects which use technology to enhance mathematical understanding and meet the guidelines for both disciplines. Students use technology as a tool to apply mathematical thinking to solve problems. Below are some ways math and technology can be integrated.

| Connection | Math | Technology |
| --- | --- | --- |
| computation | Students master basic operations with whole numbers: addition, subtraction, multiplication, division, and place holding. | Students use technology to develop mathematical concepts through application, which reinforces students' understanding of computation. |
| problem solving | Students analyze situations, formulate questions, and formulate unconventional solutions to problems. | Technology enables students to make conjectures and test them. |
| data | The use of real data enables students to make a connection between mathematics and the real world. | Students learn concepts, which they can apply in school, home, and work settings. |
| representations | Visuals, such as diagrams, graphs, and symbols, are an important part of mathematics. | Exposure to representations in technology enables students to become more comfortable with mathematical representations. |

## How We Do It

In *Across the Curriculum Math Connections,* math is integrated with technology in the following ways:

1. **Standards are identified.** Standards are met for math and technology concepts in all subject-area activities.
2. **The task and assessment are planned.** Complete step-by-step instructions and evaluation rubrics are provided for each activity.
3. **A variety of student needs are met.** Opportunities for customization are provided in each activity.
4. **Opportunities for students to communicate mathematical reasoning are available.** Technology presents many opportunities for nonstandard mathematical communication in the form of presentations, spreadsheets, and databases.
5. **Feedback is encouraged.** Activities are structured to provide students an opportunity to incorporate feedback into their projects.

# Technology in the Math Classroom

Technology can be incorporated into the math classroom in a variety of ways. Considerations include the number of computers available to students, whether the computers are available in a classroom or lab setting, and the amount of time the students are allowed per computer.

## Using Technology with *Across the Curriculum Math Connections* in the Math Classroom

1. **One-computer classrooms** can be challenging, but teachers can still provide students with meaningful experiences by using the available technology. The teacher can present material from the activities for the whole class by using a projection device and modeling the skill. It may take students longer to acquire the skills in a one-computer environment, but with planning, a teacher can provide an equitable system in which students can work.
2. **Multi-computer classrooms** allow for students to work independently or within groups. If students work on activities in groups, communication should be encouraged, but the noise level must be manageable.
3. **Computer labs** generally have enough computers for each student, but scheduling can become a challenge. Classroom teachers and technology specialists must work out a division of labor for multidisciplinary instruction. It can be effective to block-schedule math, technology, and subject-area classes so that students have extended periods to work on their activities and teachers can team teach.

## Technology Safety and Ethics

Students must be taught computer safety and ethics. Students may be familiar with classroom and playground rules but not know there are rules for using the computer.

1. **Acceptable Use** Before students are permitted to work on the computer, present and explain your school's Acceptable Use policy. If your school does not have an Acceptable Use policy, you may want to discuss implementation with your principal. Have students discuss home rules for computer use with parents or guardians.
2. **Copyright Laws** Discuss copyright laws and issues with students, and model ethical use of digital information. Teach students how to cite sources for images and text.
3. **Privacy** Explain to students that they should not look at other students' files without permission, or delete files or programs that belong to someone else.
4. **Personal Information** Students should be taught to keep personal information to themselves; they should not give out information in e-mail or on the Internet. Students should use the Internet for approved purposes only. They should use common sense and good manners when using e-mail.

# Technology Guide

## What are Computer Basics?

1. Computers store, retrieve, and process data in the form of words, numbers, or graphics. A computer can be an effective tool for organizing, editing, and filing information.
2. Computer basics are the computer skills necessary to use a computer, regardless of its particular software. In computer basics activities, students know and use proper computer terminology and learn about the computer's internal structure. Students should understand that data is saved in files and folders, and they should know how to set up new files and folders and find existing ones. Students should know how to move and manage files and folders by organizing them in meaningful ways.
3. Computer basics include evaluating and protecting computer resources as well as arranging resources so that they are easily accessible. Students can accomplish this by scanning for viruses, setting up Desktop aliases or shortcuts, and personalizing a computer's settings.

## Computer Basics in *Across the Curriculum Math Connections*

1. Before starting a computer basics activity, it may be beneficial to discuss the consequences of computer hacking, piracy, intentional virus setting, and invasion of privacy.
2. Computer Basics skills are used throughout the activities, but are represented most strongly in activities that require the creation and organization of files, and in activities that involve e-mail or Internet use.

## What is Keyboarding?

1. Keyboarding is the process of entering words or data on a keyboard. Correct keyboarding techniques will help students save time as their keying skills and speed increase.
2. Typing and keying are similar. Both methods input text with a keyboard. The alphabetical and numeric keys on the keyboard and the typewriter are arranged in a similar way. The finger positions and techniques for striking keys are the same.
3. The primary difference between keyboarding and typewriting is that typewriting puts text on paper, while keyboarding puts text into computer memory. The computer keyboard is larger because it contains computer function keys and can contain a number keypad.

## Keyboarding in *Across the Curriculum Math Connections*

1. Before starting a keyboarding activity, it may be beneficial to demonstrate proper key-tapping technique and review the correct posture and hand position for keyboarding.
2. Keyboarding skills are used throughout the activities, but are represented most strongly in activities that require text input.

## What is Word Processing?

1. Word processing is a method of writing and editing text on the computer. Students can use word processing to save time and improve the appearance of their work.
2. While most text is in the form of words and sentences, word processing programs can also manipulate numbers, symbols, graphics, tables, and equations.
3. Because word processing text resides in a computer's memory and not on paper, students easily can correct, move, and delete text. Word processing programs contain features that allow the user to select the size and style of type, check spelling, change margins, and accomplish a variety of more complex tasks.

## Word Processing in *Across the Curriculum Math Connections*

1. Before starting a word processing activity, it may be beneficial to demonstrate formatting features to students and allow students time to experiment with the word processing program.
2. Word Processing skills are used throughout the activities, but are represented most strongly in activities that require text input.

## What are Drawing and Graphics?

1. Computer graphics are images on the computer, such as photographs, clip art, and pictures that are drawn or painted.
2. Working with graphics involves inserting, moving, sizing, copying, and changing them. Students can use a program such as **Paint** or **AppleWorks** for the activities that require the use of a paint program. Your application package should be sufficient if clip art is necessary for an activity, but there are numerous clip-art packages available to purchase. You might choose to provide students with supplemental audio and video clips for activities that require multimedia.
3. The term *multimedia* refers to the use of two or more formats of media in one document. For instance, a CD-ROM book or encyclopedia that includes narration, video, and text is an example of a multimedia product.

## Drawing and Graphics in *Across the Curriculum Math Connections*

1. Before starting a drawing and graphics activity, it may be beneficial to review the drawing tools and demonstrate how to insert clip art, audio, and video into a document.
2. Drawing and Graphics skills are used throughout the activities, but are represented most strongly in activities that require clip art, illustrations, or multimedia.

# What are Gadgets?

1. Gadgets are input, output, and storage devices that are connected to a computer externally. Another term for *gadgets* is *peripherals*.
2. Input tools put information into a computer. A digital camera is an input tool; students can transfer digital photos from the camera to a hard drive. Output tools take information out of a computer. A printer is an output tool; students use a printer to transfer words and pictures from the computer's memory to a sheet of paper. Secondary storage devices, such as zip drives, let the student store information externally to save storage space on the computer's hard drive.
3. Gadgets give the computer functionality that would be impossible without the tools. The keyboard, the mouse, and the monitor are the most common input and output devices.

# Gadgets in *Across the Curriculum Math Connections*

1. Before starting a gadgets activity, it may be beneficial to demonstrate the features of the gadgets used in the activity.
2. Gadgets skills are used throughout the activities, but are represented most strongly in activities that require peripherals such as scanners, printers, and cameras.

# What is Presentation?

1. Presentation programs use slide shows to inform viewers. Slide shows can be presented to groups using a computer with a projector or interactive whiteboard, and printed copies can be distributed to an audience.
2. Presentation programs function much the same way that word processing programs do. Students write and edit text to share information, but use digital slides instead of a printed piece of paper. Students can convey ideas using words, pictures, sound, and graphic effects in a slide-show format.
3. Presentation software gives students a format in which creativity and aesthetics play an integral role in the document's design.

# Presentation in *Across the Curriculum Math Connections*

1. Before starting a presentation activity, it may be beneficial to review how to create a slide and demonstrate inserting picture and sound files onto a slide.
2. Presentation skills are used throughout the activities, but are represented most strongly in activities that require the student to present information to an audience.

## What is a Spreadsheet?

1. A spreadsheet works with math functions. A spreadsheet can calculate addition, subtraction, multiplication, and division problems that students insert as formulas. Students can save a lot of time by using a spreadsheet when they have to calculate large amounts of data.
2. A spreadsheet program manages and organizes numerical data. It performs calculations with data and can graph and chart data. Because spreadsheets automatically recalculate whenever numerical values change, they make it easy to track changes over time.
3. Students commonly use spreadsheets for the graphing function. Spreadsheet programs can graph spreadsheet data into bar, column, and line graphs, as well as into other charts and tables.

## Spreadsheets in *Across the Curriculum Math Connections*

1. Before starting a spreadsheet activity, it may be beneficial to give students an opportunity to answer questions using data from an existing spreadsheet and to demonstrate how to create and edit a spreadsheet.
2. Spreadsheet skills are used throughout the activities, but are represented most strongly in activities that require the organization of numerical information, especially in a table or graph format.

## What is a Database?

1. A database is an organized collection of related data or information. A database program is a computer application used to organize, find, and display information in different ways.
2. A computer database is made up of records, which are made up of fields. The same fields are in each record. Database users may view a database in a variety of ways; the database may look like a table, or it may look like a form to be filled in.
3. Because databases store large amounts of information, the user sees only a display of a small part of the information. In sophisticated databases a student can search and query to find certain records, or certain fields of records.

## Databases in *Across the Curriculum Math Connections*

1. Before starting a database activity, it may be beneficial to demonstrate how to find information in an existing database and how to enter information into a database.
2. Database skills are used throughout the activities, but are represented most strongly in activities that require the storage and organization of large amounts of information.

## What is Electronic Reference?

1. Electronic reference is information that is stored on a CD-ROM, a DVD, or the Internet. The information can be stored as text, pictures, or sound.
2. CD-ROM encyclopedias, dictionaries, CD-ROM books, and instructional manuals are common electronic references. Electronic references often enhance the information presented in text through the use of multimedia elements, such as narration, music, short movies, and interactive features.
3. Search features on electronic references make it quick and easy to find a desired topic within an abundance of information.

## Electronic Reference in *Across the Curriculum Math Connections*

1. Before starting an electronic reference activity, it may be beneficial to review the proper handling and use of CD-ROMs, including giving proper credit when transferring information from a CD-ROM to another software program or storage device.
2. Electronic Reference skills are used throughout the activities, but are represented most strongly in activities that require research.

## What is the Internet?

1. The Internet is a global network of computers that connects smaller networks of computers. It includes the World Wide Web, listservers, e-mail, newsgroups, and other services.
2. Computers connect to the Internet through an Internet service provider. The World Wide Web, or Web, is only one part of the Internet. The Web is made of Web pages that contain links to other Web pages. A Web page is a single page, or document, on a Web site. A Web site is all the pages, images, and files that an organization or individual makes available through the Web.
3. Because anyone can create a Web site, it is important to stress to students that not everything on the Web is appropriate or reliable.

## The Internet in *Across the Curriculum Math Connections*

1. Before starting an Internet activity, it may be beneficial to review how to access a Web page and how to use links and the **Forward** and **Back** buttons to navigate the Web.
2. Internet skills are used throughout the activities, but are represented most strongly in activities that require communication and current information.

# Educational Research for Technology

Many studies have been and are currently being conducted to test the effectiveness of educational technology initiatives. The Center for Applied Research in Educational Technology *(http://caret.iste.org)* compiles these studies.

Technology improves student performance when

- the application directly supports curriculum being assessed.
- the application provides opportunities for student collaboration.
- the application adjusts for student ability and prior experience and provides feedback to the student and teacher about student performance or progress with the application.
- the application is integrated into the typical instructional day.
- the application provides opportunities for students to design and implement projects that extend the curriculum content being assessed by a particular standardized test.
- it is used in environments where teachers, the school community, and school and district administrators support the use of technology.

In addition to the ways in which technology can influence academic performance, research studies have shown the following:

- Technology can enable the development of higher-order thinking and problem solving.
- Technology can improve student motivation, attitude, and interest in learning.
- Technology can help prepare students for the workforce.
- Technology can address the needs of low-performing, at-risk, and learning-disabled students.

# WebQuests

## WebQuest History

### Introduction to WebQuests

The **WebQuest** was developed by Bernie Dodge and Tom March at San Diego State University in 1995. It was developed as a means for teachers to use the Web in a way that is relevant to the curriculum and motivating to students. The **WebQuest** gives specific focus to material on the Web so that students can gather information without becoming lost in the vastness of the Web.

The **WebQuests** in this book follow the format outlined by Dodge and March. Each **WebQuest** in *Across the Curriculum Math Connections* contains at least six elements: an introduction, a task, sources of information in the form of URLs, a description of process, guidance in the form of questions or organizational elements, and a conclusion. Many of the **WebQuests** in this book include group activity, assigned roles or scenarios, and interdisciplinary content.

Dodge defines a **WebQuest** as "an inquiry-oriented activity in which some or all of the information that learners interact with comes from resources on the Internet, optionally supplemented with videoconferencing." He further defines a short-term **WebQuest** as one in which knowledge is acquired and integrated over one to three class periods and a long-term **WebQuest** as one in which knowledge is extended and refined over a week to a month. The instruction goals for the two types of **WebQuests** are based upon Robert Marzano's Dimensions of Thinking model. **WebQuests** in *Across the Curriculum Math Connections* can be adapted by using the **Scale UP** and **Scale BACK** features.

March outlines the features of **WebQuests** and the educational benefits. The fact that students face an authentic task and use real resources increases student motivation. Other motivators are roles within the group that require true responsibility and the fact that the answer to the central question can be presented to real people for authentic assessment. March states that **WebQuests** encourage students to engage in higher-level thinking. **WebQuests** are broken down into meaningful sections and can be constructed so that students are led through a process that models processes from expert learners. **WebQuests** also provide multiple examples and opinions so that students must derive their own understanding from the material presented and prior knowledge. Another valuable feature is the cooperative-learning aspect. Students can become "experts" in one aspect of the activity.

# WebQuest Development

## Task Types

The **Task** provides an objective and direction for the student, and as such is the most important part of a **WebQuest**. The twelve categories of tasks outlined below are defined by Dodge, who acknowledges that these categories may not cover all formats currently in existence. Dodge points out that most **WebQuests** combine two or more of the categories.

The following categories of tasks were used to create the **WebQuest** activities in *Across the Curriculum Math Connections.*

**Analytical:** Students explore relationships among variables, such as similarities and differences or cause and effect.

**Compilation:** Students put information from a variety of sources into a common format.

**Consensus Building:** Students attempt to resolve conflict over a controversial topic by allowing for, considering, and accommodating different viewpoints.

**Creative Product:** Students create a product that emphasizes creativity or self-expression within a specific format.

**Design:** Students create a product within specific constraints to meet a predetermined goal.

**Journalistic:** Students act as reporters gathering and organizing the facts surrounding an event.

**Judgment:** Students evaluate a number of choices and rank or rate them.

**Mystery:** Students explore a topic within the context of a mystery story or a puzzle.

**Persuasion:** Students attempt to convince an external audience of a particular point of view.

**Retelling:** Students report on what they have learned.

**Self-Knowledge:** Students develop a deeper understanding of themselves.

**Scientific:** Students make, test, and evaluate hypotheses.

## References

Dodge, B. (1997). Some Thoughts about WebQuests. [Online]. Available: http://webquest.sdsu/about_webquests.html [2005, April 27].

Dodge, B. (2002). WebQuest Taskonomy: A Taxonomy of Tasks. [Online]. Available: http://webquest.sdsu.edu/taskonomy.html [2005, April 27].

March, T. (1998). Why WebQuests?, an Introduction. [Online]. Available: http://ozline.com/webquests/intro.html [2005, April 27].

# Write Your Own WebQuest

After completing the **WebQuests** in *Across the Curriculum Math Connections,* you may be interested in incorporating **WebQuests** into other curriculum areas. The following process will enable you to write your own **WebQuests**.

1. **Select an appropriate topic.** Start with your curriculum. Define sections of the curriculum that have been difficult to teach well using conventional methods. Evaluate whether the topic could be explored adequately on the Web from multiple angles. The topic should require the students to use higher-level thinking skills.

2. **Select an appropriate design.** Determine the type of **Task** that best fits your topic. Download or create student and teacher templates for a design that will fit your **Task** in a Web editor such as Composer or Dreamweaver.

3. **Write the Task.** Because the **Task** contains the central question around which the **WebQuest** is designed, it is best to start writing with the **Task**. Roles and scenarios may be introduced in the **Task** if you do not plan to include these features as part of the **Introduction**. Be sure to include the central question and a description of what the students are expected to learn by completing the **WebQuest**.

4. **Write the Evaluation.** Defining the expectations for the student will help you shape the **Process** and determine appropriate resources. The **Evaluation** should present clear criteria by which students will be assessed.

5. **Write the Process.** Find the resources necessary for the completion of the **Task**. Create a set of step-by-step instructions to guide the students through the activity.

6. **Write the Introduction and Conclusion.** The **Introduction** should provide background to the student and create interest in the activity. Communicate the central idea of the **WebQuest** in this section. The **Conclusion** poses questions that enable the student to reflect upon the project and provide input.

7. **Add appropriate graphics.** Give proper credit to your sources.

8. **Publish your WebQuest.** Have students complete the **WebQuest**. Modify your **WebQuest** using information gathered from students in the **Conclusion**.

# WebQuest Planning Template

Use the following template when creating your own **WebQuests**.

### Introduction

### Task

### Resources

## Process

|   |    |   |
|---|----|---|
|   | 1. |   |
|   | 2. |   |
|   | 3. |   |
|   | 4. |   |
|   | 5. |   |
|   | 6. |   |

## Evaluation

| Criteria | 4 | 3 | 2 | 1 |
|----------|---|---|---|---|
|          |   |   |   |   |
|          |   |   |   |   |
|          |   |   |   |   |
|          |   |   |   |   |

TOTAL _____

## Conclusion

# eMathTools

The following *eMathTools* are software tools available for use with the *Real Math* program and its components. They are optional for use in *Across the Curriculum Math Connections,* but may enhance the activities for students.

## Data Organization and Display Tools

- **Spreadsheet Tool**—allows students to manage, display, sort, and calculate data. Links to the **Graphing Tool** for further data display
- **Graphing Tool**—displays data in pie charts or circle graphs, line graphs, bar graphs, or coordinate grids
- **Venn Diagram**—allows students to sort data visually

## Calculation and Counting Tools

- **Calculator**—allows students to launch a calculator to perform mathematical operations
- **Function Machine**—an electronic version of a function machine that students use to solve missing-variable problems
- **Multiplication and Division Table**—an interactive version of a table that highlights relationships between multiplication and division facts
- **Addition and Subtraction Table**—an interactive version of a table that highlights relationships between addition and subtraction facts
- **100 Table**—an interactive version of a table that highlights patterns and relationships among numbers
- **Number Line**—an electronic number line that allows students to skip count and see the relationships among whole numbers, fractions, decimals, and percentages
- **Number Stairs**—a tool to illustrate counting in units
- **Probability Tool**—uses *Number Cubes,* spinners, or tumble drums to test scenarios of probability
- **Set Tool**—allows students to visually represent and manipulative different sets of objects for a variety of counting activities
- **Base-Ten Blocks**—allows students to manipulate base-ten blocks for counting
- **Coins and Money**—uses visual representations of coins and money to represent counting
- **Fraction Tool**—represents fractional units for counting and understanding relationships
- **Array Tool**—presents arrays to represent multiplication and division patterns and relationships

## Measurement and Conversion Tools

- **Stopwatch**—measures in real time for development of counting and time concepts
- **Calendar**—an electronic calendar to develop concepts of time
- **Metric and Customary Conversion Tool**—converts metric and customary measurements in length, distance, mass and weight, time, temperature, and capacity
- **Estimating Proportion Tool**—allows visual representations of proportions to develop understanding of ratios, fractions, and decimals

## Geometric Exploration Tools

- **Tessellations**—allows students to create tessellation patterns by rotating, coloring, and tiling shapes
- **Net Tool**—allows students to manipulate 2-D shapes and then print them to create 3-D shapes
- **Shape Tools**—explores and manipulates shapes to create designs
- **Geometry Sketch Tool**—allows drawing, manipulating, and measuring a wide variety of shapes
- **Pythagorean Theorem Tool**—launches right triangles to explore the Pythagorean Theorem

# Project-Based Learning

## What It Is

Project-based learning is a process in which students mirror real-world techniques to create a product while acquiring content knowledge and skills in multiple disciplines. The teacher assigns an open-ended project, one in which more than one approach may be taken to complete the project or more than one outcome may result. Students work in cooperative groups, and the teacher assists but does not direct the learning. Generally the projects are developed over extended periods of time. Students are expected to use a variety of resources.

All of the activities in *Across the Curriculum Math Connections* are based upon project-based learning principles.

## Project-Based Learning Components in *Across the Curriculum Math Connections*

1. **Real-World Connection:** Students communicate with community members in a variety of ways or remote experts through the Internet. They may model professional practices or methods. The project should address relevant issues.
2. **Student Direction:** Students make decisions on what to research, create a management plan, resolve problems, and create a finished product. They may present the finished product and evaluate their work.
3. **Multimedia:** The use of technology reflects real-world processes, and technology tools can be integrated into planning, creating, or presentation stages of the project. Technology can also be the main focus of a project.
4. **Content:** Project content can integrate across multiple curricular areas. The project must be based upon standards of learning. Learning goals must be met through both the process and the product.
5. **Collaboration:** Students collaborate with their peers, with their teacher(s), and with members of the community. Collaboration occurs as members work on problems together, divide responsibility among group members, and provide and integrate feedback from various sources.

## Assessment for Project-Based Learning

Assessment should be incorporated early in the process so that students can evaluate themselves and adapt their project plan. *Across the Curriculum Math Connections* provides formal and informal opportunities for discussion, and incorporates multiple formats. Students do self-assessments and/or assess each other. Assessment for project-based learning can be individual, small-group, or whole-class. The criteria for assessment should be known before the project begins.

## Challenges of Project-Based Learning

1. It may be difficult to isolate the effects of problem-based learning.
2. The results of project-based learning may not be accurately assessed through standardized achievement tests.
3. As every project, and approaches within similar projects by different groups of students, differ, it may not be possible to compare results.

## Benefits of Project-Based Learning

1. **Motivation:** Students can see the real-world connection to the learning. Students develop a sense of ownership by being able to explore topics of personal interest or with preferred approaches. Students also enjoy working with their peers. Higher levels of learning are encouraged when students are able to focus on the process in self-evaluation.
2. **Equity:** Students who do not do well with traditional learning practices can excel with project-based learning. The focus is on what they know, not what they do not know. They work cooperatively, and thus do not feel singled out. Projects allow for revision and opportunities to work with a variety of technology tools.
3. **Functional Content:** Because students must respond to problems as they arise, they are invested in solving the problems instead of disregarding them because they do not understand the context.
4. **Tool Usage:** Students increase their skill with the tools but also develop the ability to discern which tool is most appropriate for the task. Students may even adapt or create their own tools as a result.

## References

Project-Based Learning. [Online] Available: http://pblchecklist.4teachers.org [2005, April 22].

Project-Based Learning with Multimedia. [Online] Available: http://pblmm.k12.ca.us/PBLGuide [2005, April 22].

# Assessment

## How to Evaluate Math

1. Math assessment should match the standards and allow students to progress at their own pace.
2. The focus of assessment should be on what the student knows, not what the student does not know.
3. Math assessment should not stress the amount of time it takes for students to complete problems or exercises.
4. Students should be aware that problems may have more than one answer.
5. Math assessment should evaluate processes in problem-based context.
6. It should demonstrate how students' work changes over time.
7. It should allow students the opportunity to demonstrate their thinking by using various communication tools, technology tools, and models.
8. Assessment should always promote student learning and not detract from instructional opportunity.

## Rubrics

A rubric is a scaled set of criteria that clearly defines for the student and the teacher what a range of acceptable and unacceptable performances looks like. A rubric provides students with expectations about what will be assessed, as well as standards that need to be met. Using rubrics to evaluate math increases consistency in the rating of performance, production, and understanding.

Rubrics are provided for every activity in *Across the Curriculum Math Connections.* A rubric template is provided on page 156 if you would like to develop your own rubric for an activity. A presentation rubric is provided on page 157 so that you can evaluate organization, content, and presentation skills if students present their activities.

If you choose to develop your own rubric, consider the qualities or features by which you can determine if the student has produced an excellent response to the assessment task. Once you have related the task to specific goals for students, you must evaluate what the students must do to show that they are working toward or achieving those goals. Outline expectations for each task. It is helpful to have samples or models of student work that exemplify the criteria you might use in judging each task. Students should see and understand the rubric before completing the task.

## Portfolios

A portfolio is a collection of a student's work that exhibits the student's planning, progress, and problem-solving skills in many areas of math. The use of portfolios encourages collective assessment and focuses on students' strengths instead of weaknesses. It builds self-esteem in students through successes with a collection of work and develops strong work habits in students. Portfolio assessment, self assessment, and peer assessment guidelines are provided on pages 153–155.

# Portfolio Assessment

**Name** _____

**Date** _____

**Project** _____

Did you accomplish your goals with this project? _____

Would you choose this project for your portfolio? Why or why not? _____

_____

_____

_____

_____

What do you like about this project? _____

_____

_____

_____

_____

What did you learn from doing this project? _____

_____

_____

_____

_____

_____

_____

# Self Assessment

Name _____

Date _____

Project _____

**Describe:** What did you do to participate in the project? _____

_____

_____

_____

_____

**Analyze:** How did your participation reveal or connect with the goals of the project? _____

_____

_____

_____

**Interpret:** How did your participation in this project relate to real life? _____

_____

_____

_____

_____

**Decide:** Was your participation effective, or could it be improved? How? _____

_____

_____

_____

_____

_____

# Peer Assessment

Name _____

Date _____

Project _____

**Describe:** What role did this student play in the project? _____
_____
_____
_____

**Analyze:** How did this student help the group meet the goals of the project? _____
_____
_____
_____

**Interpret:** How could this student work with other members of the group? _____
_____
_____
_____

**Decide:** Was this student's participation effective, or could it be improved? _____
_____
_____
_____

# Project Rubric

Name _____

Date _____

Project _____

| Criteria | 4 | 3 | 2 | 1 |
|---|---|---|---|---|
|  |  |  |  |  |
|  |  |  |  |  |
|  |  |  |  |  |
|  |  |  |  |  |

TOTAL _____

## Directions

Make a copy of the blank rubric. Fill in criteria based upon objectives in the first column. Write a description of traits for each objective in each row, ranging from the highest level of expectation to minimum expectation. Use unique descriptors. Copy and distribute the rubric to students.

# Presentation Rubric

Name _____

Date _____

Project _____

| Criteria | 3 | 2 | 1 |
|---|---|---|---|
| Organization | Clear direction throughout the presentation. Captures attention at onset. Details build to main point and are appropriate to the subject. Provokes thought. | Order of presentation makes sense, and there is a clear beginning, middle, and end. Most of the details are in the correct place. | Order is confusing. Beginning and end are not clearly defined. Limited detail. |
| Content | Central idea is focused, clear, and specific. | Stays on topic. Central idea is obvious. | Strays from topic. Central idea is undeveloped. |
| Presentation | Unique, insightful, or fresh approach. Presenter is confident and clear. | Successful but ordinary approach. Presenter is earnest. | Unreflective and routine approach. Presenter seems indifferent. |

TOTAL _____

**ACROSS THE CURRICULUM Math Connections • Assessment**

# Answer Key

|  | Math | Subject Area | Technology |  | Math | Subject Area | Technology |
|---|---|---|---|---|---|---|---|
| **Chapter 1** |  |  |  | **Chapter 7** |  |  |  |
| Activity 2 | B | F | N | Activity 2 | D | H | N |
| **Chapter 2** |  |  |  | **Chapter 8** |  |  |  |
| Activity 1 | C | J | K | Activity 1 | D | F | N |
| **Chapter 3** |  |  |  | **Chapter 9** |  |  |  |
| Activity 2 | C | G | K | Activity 2 | B | F | L |
| **Chapter 4** |  |  |  | **Chapter 10** |  |  |  |
| Activity 1 | C | F | L | Activity 1 | D | F | L |
| **Chapter 5** |  |  |  | **Chapter 11** |  |  |  |
| Activity 1 | B | J | L | Activity 1 | A | G | K |
| **Chapter 6** |  |  |  | **Chapter 12** |  |  |  |
| Activity 2 | C | J | L | Activity 2 | C | G | N |

**PLAN Answers**

**Chapter 3** Activity 2 Students should circle the illustration of the aphid.